sashiko

sashiko

20 projects using traditional Japanese stitching

JILL CLAY

contents

Introduction

Sashiko is pronounced *sash(i)ko*, the *i* being almost silent. It means 'little stabs' because it involves stabbing the needle in and out of the fabric, to make a number of small gathers on the needle. When the needle is pulled through it creates a series of small stitches. It has also sometimes been called 'rice stitch' because in its traditional yarn colour of off-white, it resembles a grain of rice.

It is a mystery as to exactly when sashiko began, although it is thought to be centuries ago, but it certainly grew in Japan out of necessity. As fabrics were all hand produced from spinning to weaving, it was precious and had to last as long as possible. So, once clothing was past its best it was remade by cutting out the good sections of fabric, then mended, strengthened and patched using sashiko stitching. Clothing was also insulated using sashiko stitching: fabrics were layered and stitched together with sashiko – the fabric in the best condition would be on the top – with successive layers there for added warmth.

During the winter months, while outside work was limited, Japanese women practised sashiko. Later it was even used to judge a woman's suitability for marriage. It became an integral part of a manual labourer's wife's skill, so was passed down through the generations.

As with many crafts born from necessity, those with an artistic flair soon started to add patterns. Designs differed throughout Japan, with many including auspicious motifs and patterns from Buddhism. Today, sashiko stitching is still used but it is mainly for decorative purposes. People create their own unique designs or use traditional patterns as the basis for new ones.

Several sashiko designs with an interesting history or symbolism are used for the projects in this book, including:

Shippo Tsunagi (see page 120) Also known as Seven Treasures, this design has long been used in Buddhist art. The seven treasures of Buddha are gold, silver, agate, pearl, coral, lapis and crystal or amber.

Fundo Isanagi (see page 114) Everyday objects were used as the inspiration for sashiko. Fundou are counterweights used on balancing scales.

Hishi Seigaiha (see page 116) This design dates back to Persia. It has become one of the best-known designs in sashiko.

Bamboo (see page 108) The bamboo design signifies prosperity as well as purity and strength.

Asanoha (see page 109) The hemp leaf was used in designs as a good luck charm for surviving winter, just as the hemp leaf did. It is also often used on children's clothing in the hope that the child will grow as strong as the hemp plant.

Noshi (see page 110) This symbol signifies good fortune. With this design, you can stitch just the outline or fill in each ribbon with a different pattern.

Maneki Neko (see page 113) The Maneki Neko (beckoning cat) is a good luck charm that's widely used throughout Asia.

Although there are some 'rules' to sashiko, I prefer to think of them as guidelines, which is just what my sashiko teacher taught me. Following the guidelines is important, but so is enjoying what you are doing. The simple message is don't take it too seriously, relax and enjoy.

Jill Clay

Getting started

Tools and materials

One of the wonderful things about sashiko is that you don't have to buy lots of tools and materials. The essentials are just a needle, thread and fabric. You can also take it with you wherever you travel without the need for frames and hoops – a small pouch or drawstring bag can hold hours of sewing.

Sashiko fabric

Sashiko was traditionally stitched on indigo, hemp and cotton. Indigo was primarily used because it was readily available and considered hardwearing. It was even thought to repel insects and snakes. It is unlikely that most of what we think of as indigo is 'true indigo'; however, modern techniques can produce wonderful indigo-coloured fabric.

Nowadays, a multitude of fabrics is used for sashiko. The most important feature is for the fabric to have an even weave. This simply means that the warp and weft threads are the same thickness and distance apart.

Pre-printed sashiko fabrics are also readily available (see below). Once the stitching is finished, they can simply be rinsed with warm water to remove the printed guidelines.

Patterned fabrics, such as checks and stripes, work well for sashiko, as they provide lines to follow. You can also sew onto pre-made items, such as jeans, jackets and bedding.

Because of the rainbow of thread colours available, you can use any shade of fabric. Blue and white always looks more traditional, but experiment to see what effect you like best.

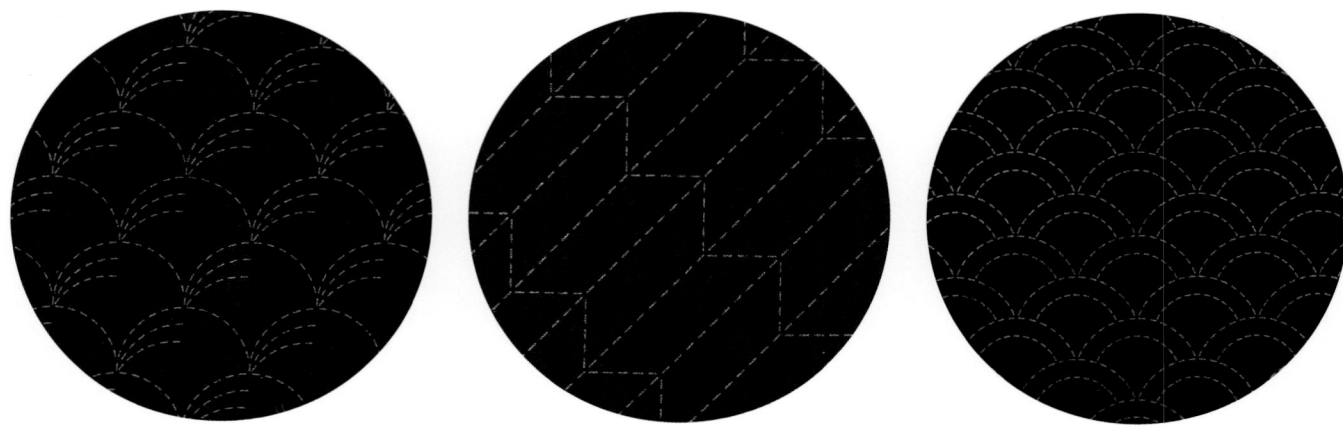

Pattern transferring equipment

There are various methods you can use to transfer sashiko patterns to fabric. These are explained on pages 16–17. You can choose whichever you feel most comfortable doing, or is most suitable for the project. Depending on the method you choose, you may need:

- Temporary fabric markers (see right)
- Permanent fine liner pen
- Light or featherweight fusible interfacing or water-soluble interfacing
- Tracing paper or greaseproof paper
- Chaco paper (Japanese carbon paper)
- Quilting mat or large piece of cardboard
- Small clips, such as quilting clips

TEMPORARY FABRIC MARKERS

There are several types of temporary fabric marker available, including chalk pens, tailor's chalk and quilter's pencils. They are suitable for most fabrics and come in a good range of colours. However, make sure you always test the fabric marker on the particular fabric you want to use.

Hera

A hera is a traditional Japanese sewing marker. Originally made from bone, they are now made from plastic. The curved tool (shown below) scores across the fabric and leaves a polished line. It is particularly good on darker fabric and washes away easily. It's ideal for designs with straight lines, but it's not the best for very large projects as the lines will disappear with handling and may have to be redrawn.

Erasable pens

These are a great tool, but make sure you read the manufacturer's instructions, as some are water-erasable while others are removed with heat. If using one on a light-coloured fabric, be aware that with some brands of pen the lines can reappear with changes in temperature, so testing is important.

Sashiko needles

You can use embroidery needles or crewel needles for sashiko, but dedicated sashiko needles are longer and will therefore enable you to gather more stitches on them. Sashiko needles are available in shorter lengths, too, and these are useful for handling curves. They also come in different thicknesses: Japanese handmade needles are relatively thin compared to the mass-produced type, and as they have smaller eyes they are only suited to finer threads. Always choose your needle to match your threads and fabric weight: using a thinner needle with a thicker fabric will make stitching more difficult than using a thicker, longer needle; likewise, trying to sew thinner threads with a long, thick needle will be less easy.

Sashiko thread

Sashiko thread has a medium twist and is made from very strong, hardwearing cotton. Historically, sashiko thread was always an off-white colour. Once dyeing and bleaching techniques developed, colour ranges expanded. It now comes in various weights and a multitude of colours, both plain and variegated. Hand-dyed threads are particularly lovely. Note that if you buy variegated thread, make sure the colour variations are quite close in shade to each other; if they're not, you may not achieve the graduated look you're after.

TIP
······

The eye of a needle has two different sides: one is flat, the other is bevelled. If one side is difficult to thread, spin round and try the other side.

TIP
······

Keeping the paper band that comes with most threads and tying a little bit of thread onto it is a great way to ensure you can repeat the exact colours should you run out.

Backing fabrics and wadding (batting)

Several of the projects will require a backing fabric and wadding. When choosing a backing fabric, always consider the project it will be used for. Choose a natural fibre, such as muslin, which is available in various weights, or re-use fabric from old clothes and bedlinen. Test the fabric before starting your project, to make sure it is easy to stitch through.

Do a little research into which wadding would be most suitable for the project you're making. Wadding can vary from manufacturer to manufacturer and this can affect how it will behave.

Other necessary items

To complete the projects in this book, make sure you also have to hand the following:

- Sewing machine
- Sewing needle and thread
- Dressmaking scissors
- Small embroidery scissors or snips
- Pins
- Fabric glue
- Clear tape
- Iron and ironing board
- Plain paper
- Knitting needle or chopstick (for pushing sewn corners through)
- Tape measure
- Ruler
- Pair of compasses

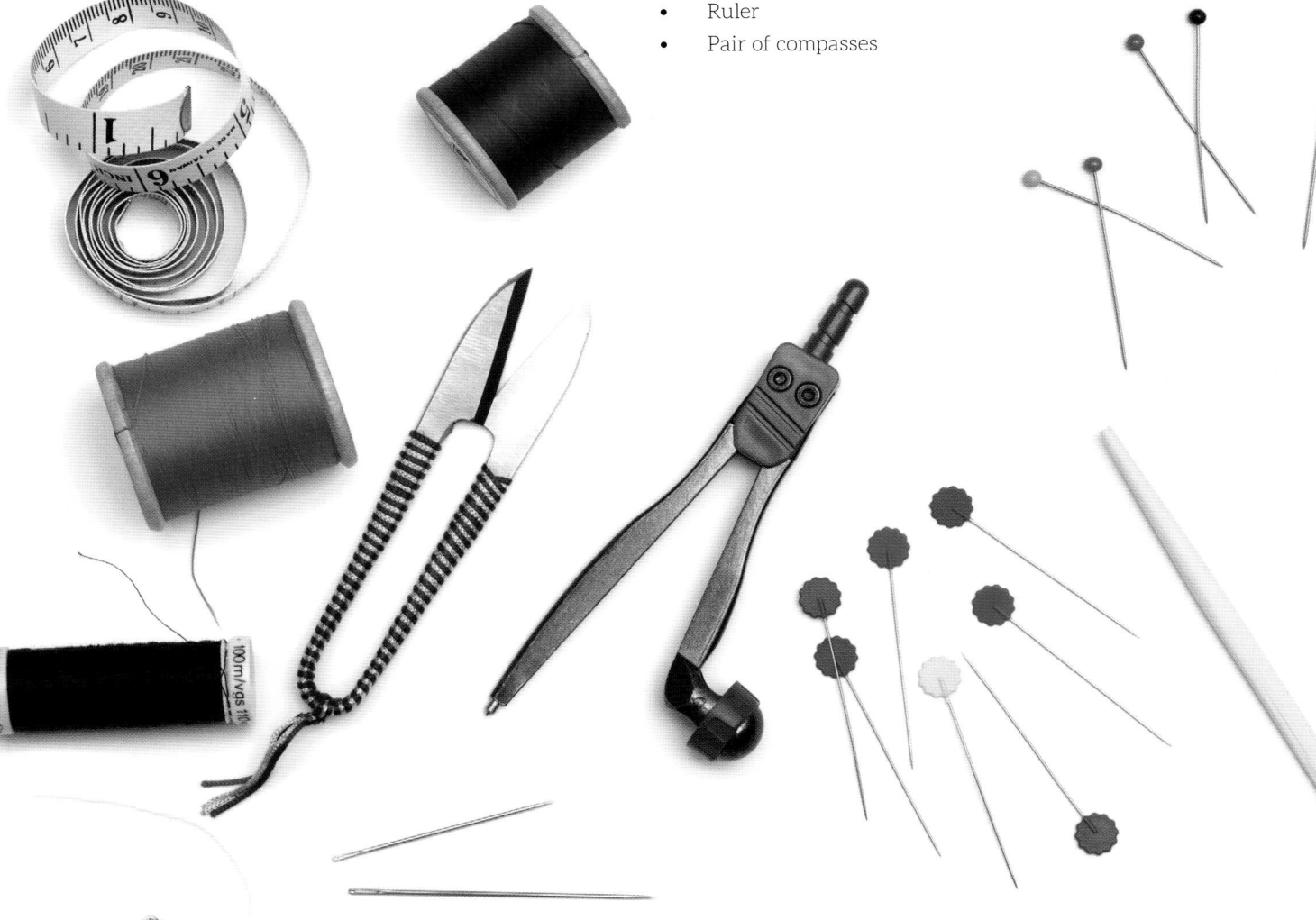

Techniques

Sashiko is quite a simple process – there are just a few techniques for you to master. Firstly, if you wish to use fabric that is not pre-marked with a pattern, you'll need to learn how to transfer a pattern to your chosen fabric. There are plenty of traditional sashiko patterns, of which you'll find several within the Pattern Library at the back of the book, but you can also create your own designs. Once a pattern is transferred to your fabric, you'll need to know how to complete the sashiko stitching. You'll find all this information, plus guidance on making up the projects, on the following pages.

Sashiko patterns

On pages 104–131 there is a Pattern Library containing the templates for many traditional sashiko patterns as well as some of the other designs that are used in the projects. You can easily enlarge or reduce the templates by scanning them into a computer then changing their size using basic design software. Alternatively, most libraries will have a copier machine and staff that can help. Once they are at the size you require, you will need to use one of the methods explained on pages 16–17 to transfer them to your fabric.

USING YOUR OWN SASHIKO PATTERNS

Instead of using the templates from the Pattern Library, you may like to create your own designs. When you first start drawing designs, geometric shapes are by far the easiest to work with. Don't run before you can walk, though. Choose relatively easy shapes. Curved shapes, for instance, are best attempted once you've had some experience.

You can design using any shape of grid. Try this if you have a computer. Make a grid of 4 squares x 5 squares. Create diagonal lines across the individual squares. Group all of the lines together and save the diagram (1). Now you can copy and paste the diagram when you want to use it. Manipulating the width and height of the diagram can give you many extra pattern options (2), (3). If you do not have a computer, simply use graph paper (see pages 132–134) and draw different sizes of grids with either squares or rectangles. Once you have got used to squares you can start playing with other shapes like circles and hearts (4). There are no limits to the designs you can produce.

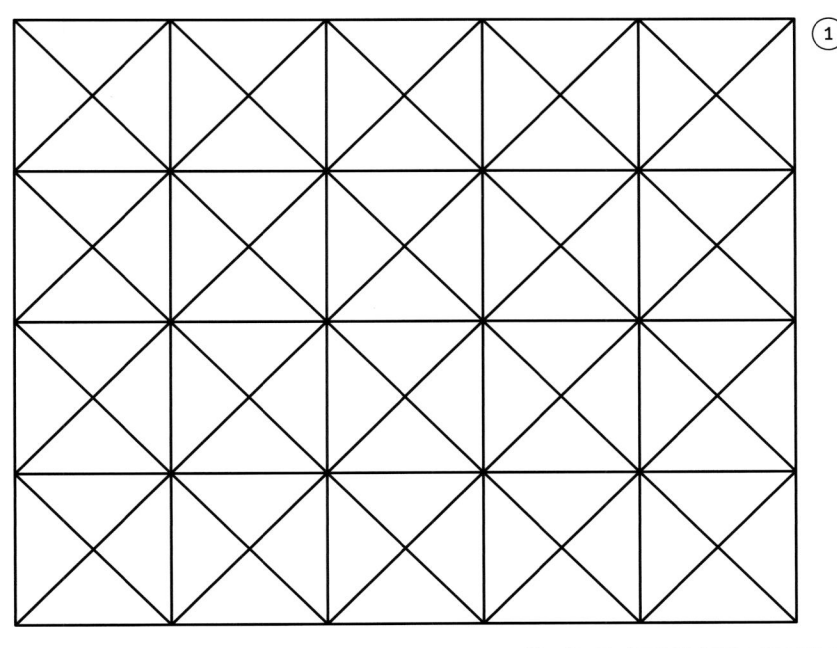

①

TIP
......
Keep your designs
and photocopy them.
You can add to them
later, or scan them into
your computer and use
an easy design program
to distort the patterns.

②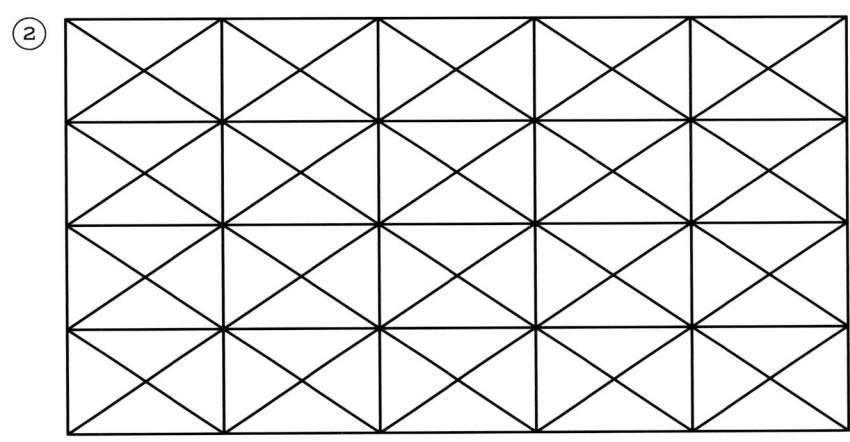

③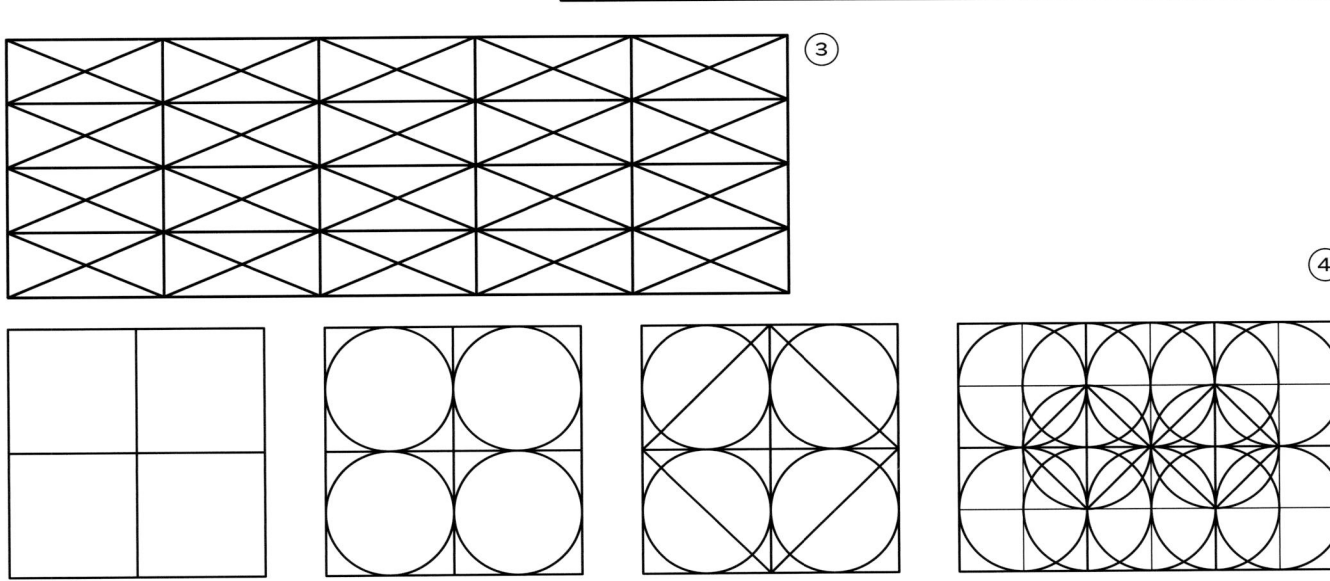

④

Transferring sashiko patterns to fabric

If you feel confident enough to do it, a repeat straight-line design can be drawn directly onto light fabrics with a ruler and water/heat erasable pen, or with a chalk pen or tailor's chalk onto darker fabric. But there are also several easy methods to transfer sashiko designs onto fabric, as follows.

CHACO PAPER

Chaco paper is Japanese dressmaker's carbon paper. Draw your design onto plain paper. Place the Chaco between your fabric and your drawn design. I like to hold all three pieces together with small quilting clips – this keeps them steady when tracing, but also allows you to open it up and check your lines. Work on a quilting mat or cardboard and trace over your design with a sharp pencil or hera (see page 11).

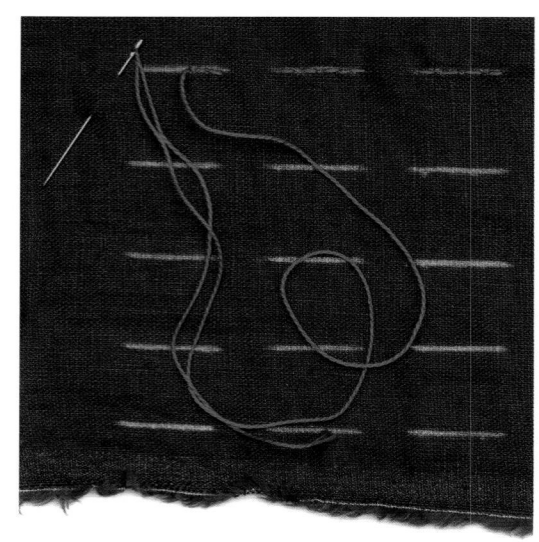

TIP
......
Before using any of the methods described here it is better to test them on a small area of your fabric to make sure that the lines can be removed successfully. If your design is very intricate, you may have to reapply the lines after a few hours of work.

TIP
......
Always test which is the correct side of Chaco paper to use and mark it for future use.

TRACING PAPER / GREASEPROOF PAPER

Draw or trace your design onto tracing paper or greaseproof paper and tack it onto the fabric. Stitch the design and, when finished, remove the tacking stitches and carefully tear away the tracing paper. This is a particularly good method if you're working on wool or felt fabric, as they're not so easy to draw on.

INTERFACING

It's easy to transfer your designs using light or featherweight fusible interfacing. The interfacing remains on your fabric, so make sure you choose the correct weight for your project and use permanent pens, which will only leave marks on the back of your work.

Lightly tape your design to a flat surface or, if available, to a lightbox. Place the glued side of the interfacing down on top of your design. Trace through using a permanent fine liner. Fuse the interfacing to the reverse of your fabric, using the directions provided by the manufacturer. Place a piece of scrap fabric between your iron and the interfacing before ironing. That way there is less chance of it spoiling your fabric should you accidentally have your fusible side the wrong way up.

Water-soluble interfacing

This type of interfacing is ironed onto your fabric and, once you have finished stitching, can be washed away. Make sure you follow the manufacturer's instructions, as not all brands work in the same way.

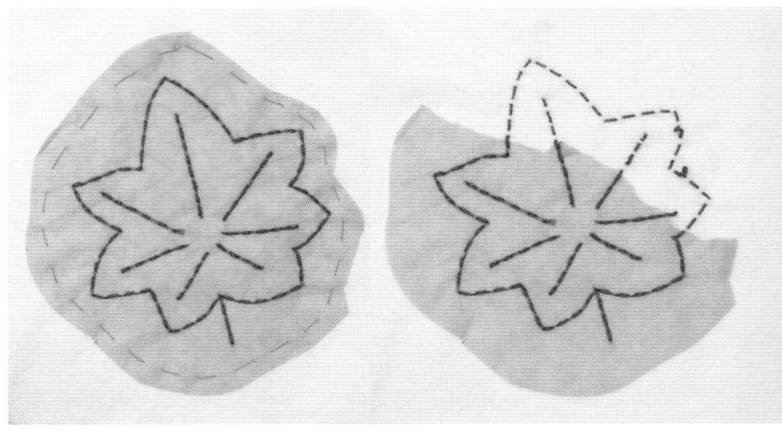

TIP
······

Reverse your design prior to transferring to your interfacing, so it will be the correct way round on the right side of the sashiko.

Using sashiko thread

Carefully open up the skein and find the place where the thread is tied together. Open up the full loop and cut through the tied area, cutting through all the threads in one snip. Your threads will be about 38in (96cm) long. As this is very long, it may be a little strange to work with at first, but after a while you'll get used to it.

After you have threaded your needle, hold the thread and let the needle drop. This will take out any extra twists you may have created by threading it.

Once you own several colours of thread, you will need to keep them tidy. Spending an hour untangling threads is not a great way to relax! A good idea is to take a piece of any thread and tie all of your threads together at one end. Split them into three and plait the threads to the bottom. Tie another piece of thread at the bottom. Some people will pull a thread from one end. This works, of course, but I prefer to hold both ends of the plait in one hand and pull out the threads from the middle. Add new threads by simply undoing the plait, adding your new thread and re-plaiting.

SINGLE THREAD VS DOUBLE THREAD

The choice between single and double thread is dependent on your project and, of course, personal preference. The vast majority of projects here are stitched with single thread.

SINGLE THREAD

- Easy to pass through your fabric.
- Thread lasts twice as long as double.
- Less texture.
- Very easy to undo stitches that need changing, as you can simply remove the needle.

DOUBLE THREAD

- More difficult to pass through, especially on heavier fabrics.
- Uses twice as much thread.
- Fabric becomes much stronger with a great deal of surface texture.
- As threads are joined, it is difficult to undo mistakes.

TIP
......
Make sure you don't split the threads. Use a needle threader to avoid this happening.

TIP
......
Add a small loop of thread to the item you intend to stitch onto. Wash the item and check the thread for any bleeding.

Sewing sashiko

In sashiko, you do not hold the work in a hoop or stretcher. Several stitches are worked at one time, folding the fabric into pleats as you insert the needle.

STARTING AND FINISHING STITCHING

You can either make a knot in your thread before you begin, or start without a knot, which is preferable if both sides of the work are visible. A knot is the stronger method of starting and, if it is small and tight, can be almost invisible and hidden in the seams. The quilter's knot when pulled tight is both neat and strong. Wrap the end of the thread around the needle twice and pull through ①.

To start without a knot, sew a few stitches in the opposite direction to which you will be stitching. Turn the work and sew over the same stitches, stitching through the thread to hold it in place ②.

When finishing a length of thread or starting a new one, take the needle to the back of the fabric and weave the thread through some of the stitches you have already sewn. You should do this with no less than six stitches to stop the work from unravelling ③.

With items that are worn and washed regularly, you should finish your stitching with a small knot as well as weaving through the back of threads. Take your needle to the back and wrap the thread around it once as close as you can to the fabric. Hold the needle between your forefinger and thumb, so that the knot can't travel. Slowly pull the needle through, keeping the knot close to the fabric. You will need at least 2in (5cm) of thread to do this ④.

TIP
······

To protect your fabric from fraying, stitch a row of small stitches around the edge. If possible, do this on a sewing machine. By making the line ¼in (6mm) on all sides, you won't only protect your fabric from fraying but also have a guide showing where to end your sewing line.

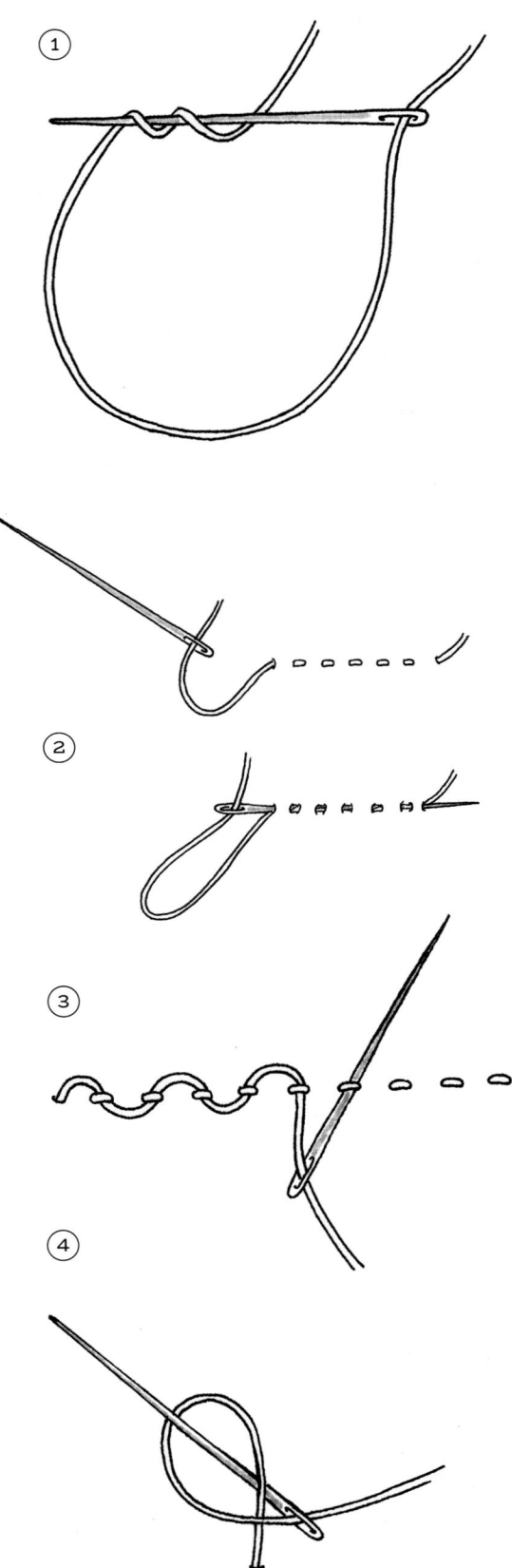

① ② ③ ④

BASIC STITCHES

Running stitch

The main stitch that you will use for sashiko is running stitch. Weave the needle back and forth through the fabric several times, then pull the thread through and smooth out the fabric to produce a number of stitches in one go 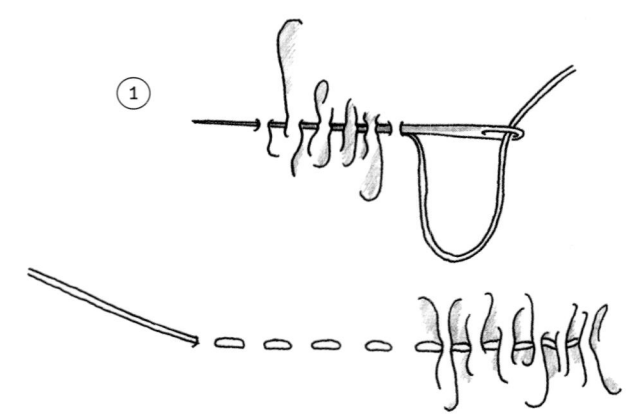.

A good rule to follow is to make the stitch the size of a grain of rice. The proportion used for the stitching should be 3:2. Three is the proportion for the length of the stitch (on the right side of the fabric) and two is the proportion for the space between the stitches. However, when stitching on the wrong side of the fabric, such as when following a design traced onto interfacing (see page 17), the proportions should be reversed, so the stitch length is two and the space between is three. When the sashiko is turned to the right side, the size of the stitches and gaps will be correct.

Bridging stitches

Throughout your sashiko you will need to jump from one area of stitching to another. If using pre-printed fabric you should find that nothing contained in the pattern is too big a gap. If you do need to jump between areas of work, bridging stitches are a neat and secure way to do this.

To jump over a gap in the centre of your work, simply make a longer stitch on the reverse side of the fabric 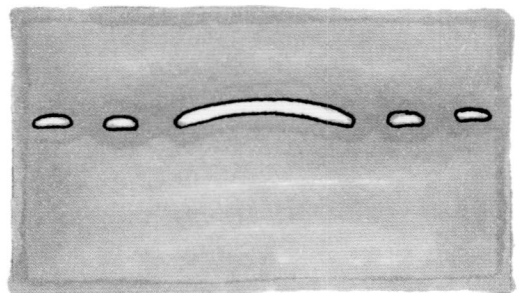.

To bridge large gaps, work along the edge of your fabric where it will not be seen in the finished item. Place a small stitch into the edge of your fabric, go through to the back of the fabric and form a long loose bridging stitch 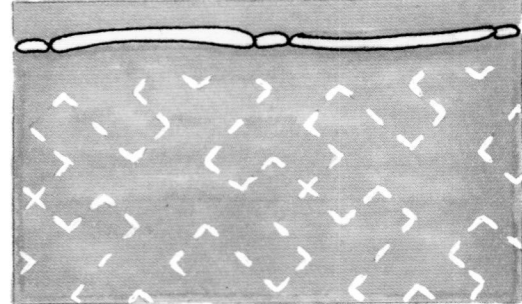. You can repeat the process with small stitches followed by longer stitches to bridge a larger gap. The ideal length for the longer stitches is no more than 1in (2.5cm) to keep the threads from tangling.

Bridging stitches are not pulled tight – they have a little extra thread left in each one to maintain your tension. You then have the security of knowing that you can adjust your tension later, if you need to, without unpicking.

TIP
······

If you have to unpick stitches, hold the fabric tightly between finger and thumb at the last correct stitch. Use the eye end of the needle, not the sharp end, to avoid splitting threads.

Making up instructions

Use basic hand stitching or a sewing machine to make up your pieces.

SLIPSTITCH ①

A slipstitch, or ladder stitch, is an easy way to sew a seam from the outside of a garment or item. Working on the right side of the fabric, make a stitch at the seam line of one side of the opening and then work a stitch in the other side. After two or three stitches, pull to close.

APPLIQUÉ STITCH ②

Appliqué stitch, or blanket stitch, is a method of adding one piece of fabric on to the top of another piece of fabric to create layers. Pin the fabric piece on top of the main panel. Insert the needle through the two layers and out through the main panel at the edge of the top fabric layer. Keep the thread under the point of the needle and draw the needle up to tighten the thread to finish the stitch. Keep the stitches evenly spaced and equal in length.

TURNING THROUGH ③

Turning through simply means stitching seams on the reverse side of an item, but leaving a gap large enough to turn the fabric through so that it is right side out. It is a good idea to reinforce the edges of the turning gap with a couple of extra stitches to avoid the chance of it splitting open as you pull the fabric through.

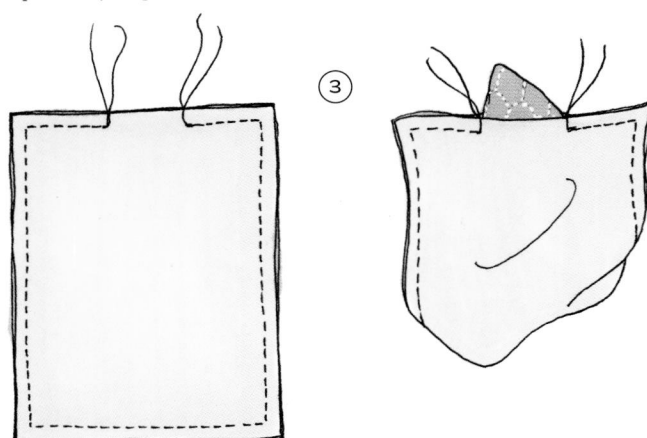

PRESSING ④

It is worth placing a cloth over your stitches before pressing them with an iron. Use a low to medium heat setting.

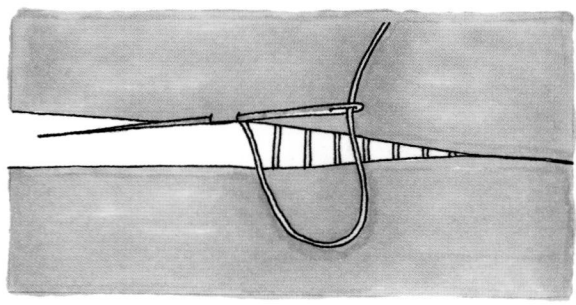

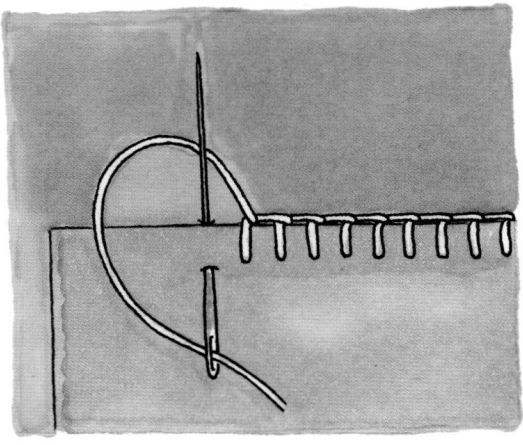

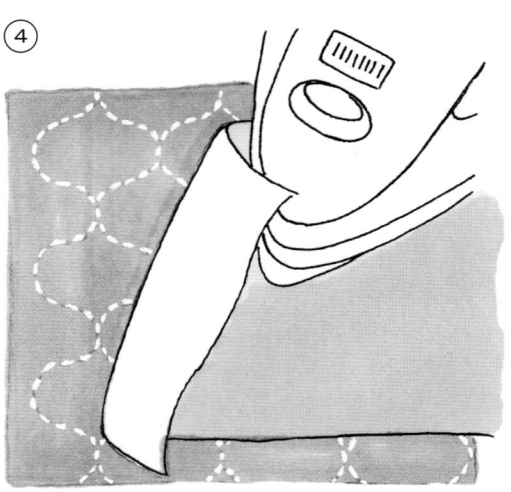

The projects

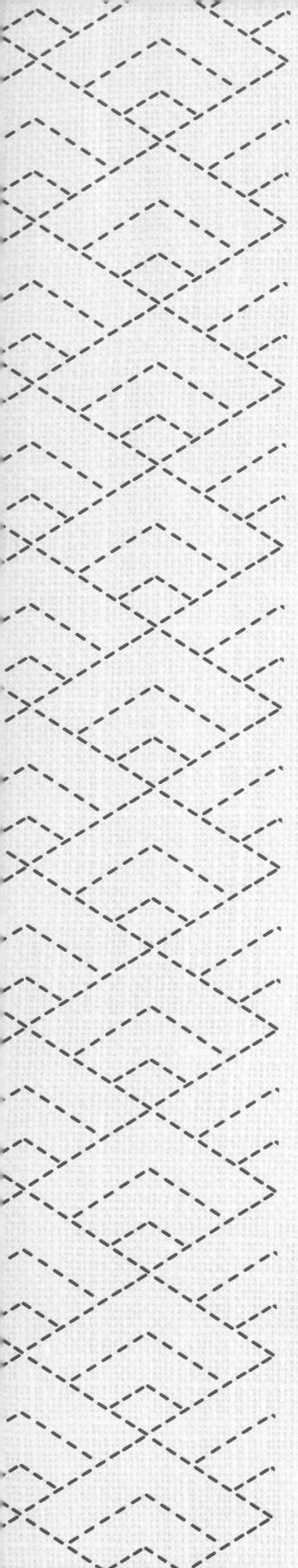

Greetings cards

YOU WILL NEED

- Sashiko fabric
- Pattern transferring equipment (see page 11)
- Sashiko needle and thread
- Scissors
- Blank card, with or without an aperture
- Fabric glue
- Iron-on stabilizer (optional)

TIP
......

Alternative uses for sashiko samples are appliqué patches, coasters, bag panels or quilting blocks.

While learning sashiko, you will most likely end up with lots of small sample pieces of fabric. Samples are a perfect way to test out new patterns and different colour combinations. They are also ideal for using up short pieces of thread. They can be kept as a record of your improvement, or they can be used to make greetings cards like these.

For the sashiko patterns shown here, use the templates on page 104. Alternatively, you can select a different pattern from the Pattern Library (see pages 104–131) or design your own (see pages 14–15). Transfer the pattern to the sashiko fabric (see pages 16–17) and complete the stitching (see page 20).

Cut around the design, allowing a ½in (1.2cm) margin all around, then simply glue it to the inside of a blank card behind the aperture. If you have an odd-sized sample that you want to mount onto a card, and it doesn't fit into a conventionally sized aperture card, then you can back it with iron-on stabilizer, cut around the edges and glue it to the front of a plain card.

To create a fringed edging around the sample, as shown on the facing page, make sure you have a fabric that has the same thickness of threads in both directions, warp and weft. Use a needle to gently pull out a thread on each side of the sample, one at a time, until you have the desired depth of fringe.

Brooch

YOU WILL NEED

- Two-part brooch
- Pen and paper (optional)
- Pattern transferring equipment (see page 11)
- Sashiko fabric
- Sashiko needle and thread
- Pencil with eraser tip
- Scissors
- Fabric glue
- Wadding (optional)

TIP
......

If the fabric you are using is thin, you can place a little wadding between it and the brooch back.

For the sashiko patterns shown here, use the templates on page 104. Alternatively, you can select a different pattern from the Pattern Library (see pages 104–131) and reduce it to fit the brooch (see page 14) or take a piece of paper, draw around the brooch insert (the part of the brooch that sits inside the outer casing), and create your own design. Transfer your chosen pattern to the sashiko fabric (see pages 16–17) and complete the stitching (see page 20).

Cut around the design, allowing a margin of approximately ¼–⅜in (6–10mm) for folding around the back of the brooch insert. Make little cuts into the edges of the fabric to help it fold neatly. Make sure the cuts stop slightly short of the size of the brooch back.

Place the fabric right side down onto a flat surface. Place the brooch insert right side down onto the fabric and hold it down with the eraser end of a pencil. Cover the reverse of the brooch insert with strong glue and let the glue dry to tacky. Fold a tab over on the top, bottom, left and right sides of the fabric, then fold over the rest of the tabs around the edge and attach to the glue. Holding the brooch with the pencil makes this easier. Work your way around the brooch insert, making sure it stays precisely in place.

Once you are happy with the positioning and the glue is dry you can fill the bevelled brooch back with glue and carefully place the brooch insert right side up into the cavity. Press down firmly and allow to dry.

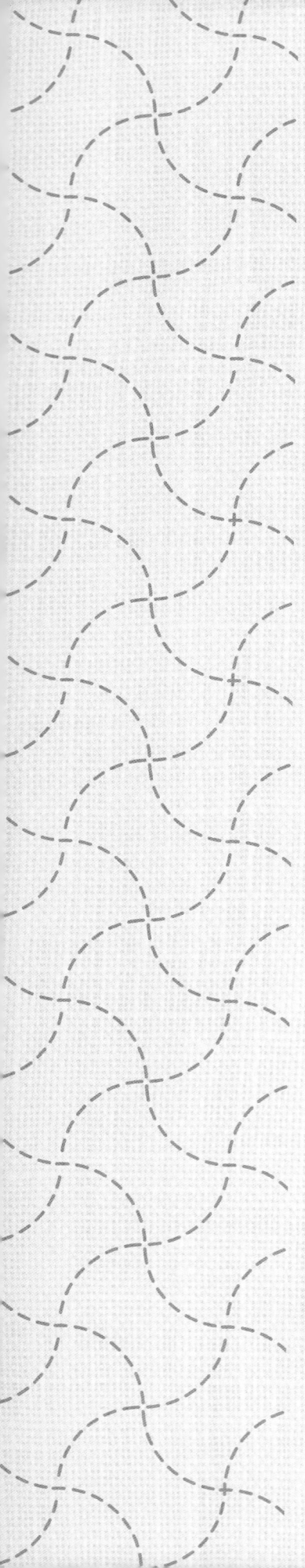

Tablemats

YOU WILL NEED

- Tape measure
- Colourfast and washable sashiko fabric: 10 x 13¼in (25.4 x 33.6cm) for each tablemat
- Pattern transferring equipment (see page 11)
- Sashiko needle and thread
- Sewing machine/needle and thread
- Backing fabric
- Chopstick or knitting needle
- Iron

For the sashiko pattern shown here, use the template provided on page 105. Alternatively, you can select a different pattern from the Pattern Library (see pages 104–131) or design your own (see pages 14–15). Transfer the pattern to your sashiko fabric (see pages 16–17) and complete the stitching (see page 20).

Place the backing fabric and the sashiko fabric right sides together and stitch around the edge, leaving a ¼in (6mm) seam allowance. Leave a 2in (5cm) gap on one edge. Turn through the gap and use a chopstick or knitting needle to push the corners out as neatly as possible from inside the panel.

Finally, slipstitch (see page 21) or machine sew the gap and press to finish.

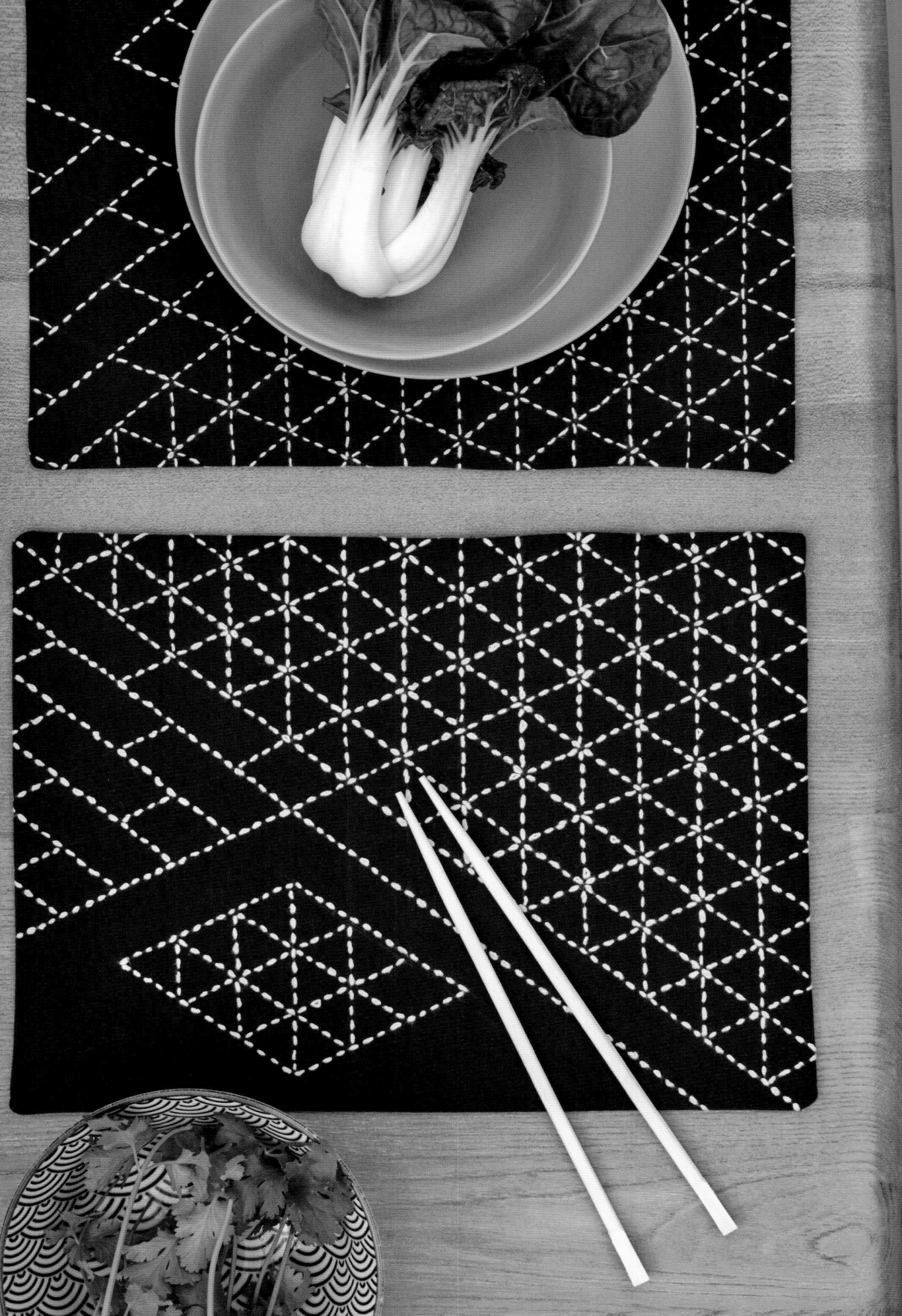

Traditional sashiko design shown here:
FUNDO ISANAGI (see page 114).

Coasters

YOU WILL NEED

- Colourfast and washable sashiko fabric: 10 x 10in (25.4 x 25.4cm), either pre-printed or your own choice of plain fabric

- Fabric marker

- Pattern transferring equipment (see page 11)

- Sashiko needle and thread

- Fabric scissors

- Patterned edging fabric of a similar weight to the main fabric, such as cotton or cotton/linen blend: 8 pieces, 1¼ x 5in (3.2 x 12.7cm); 8 pieces, 1¼ x 6½in (3.2 x 16.5cm)

- Thin wadding: 4 pieces, 6½ x 6½in (16.5 x 16.5cm)

- Backing fabric of a similar weight to the main fabric, such as cotton or cotton/linen blend: 4 pieces, 6½ x 6½in (16.5 x 16.5cm)

- Sewing machine/needle and thread

- Chopstick or knitting needle

- Iron

If sewing multiple items such as coasters, it is easier to complete the stitching on one piece of fabric rather than many small pieces. Once the sewing is completed, the individual coasters are then simply cut out.

Mark the sashiko fabric into four 5 x 5in (12.7 x 12.7cm) sections. Mark a ¼in (6mm) seam allowance around the edges of each of the four sections (see the template on page 32).

If you're not using pre-printed fabric, use the template to transfer the design to plain fabric. Alternatively, select a pattern from the Pattern Library (see pages 104–131) or design your own (see pages 14–15), then transfer the pattern (see pages 16–17) into the four squares.

TIP
......

For the backing and edging, choose a fabric that can either blend with or contrast your main fabric. This can be any fabric that is a similar weight to the main fabric to be stitched.

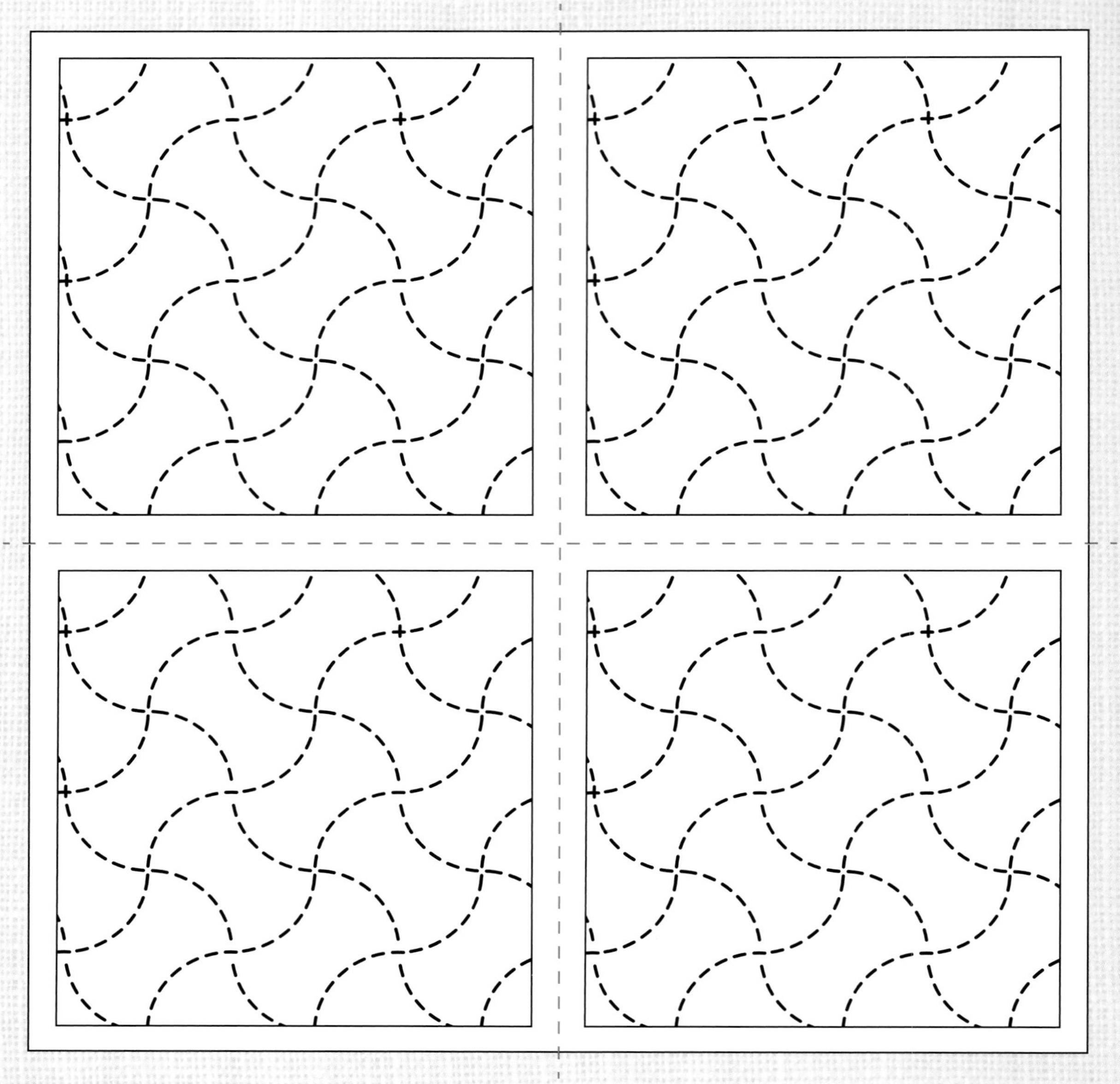

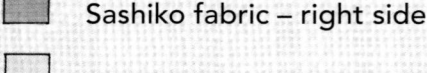

Sashiko fabric – right side

Sashiko fabric – wrong side

Edging fabric – right side

Edging fabric – wrong side

Backing fabric – right side

Backing fabric – wrong side

Wadding

TEMPLATE FOR COASTERS
Enlarge by 150%

Complete the stitching inside the seam allowances
of the four squares (see page 20) ①.

Cut along the first set of marked lines, shown in red
broken lines on the template, to give you four 5 x 5in
(12.7 x 12.7cm) pieces.

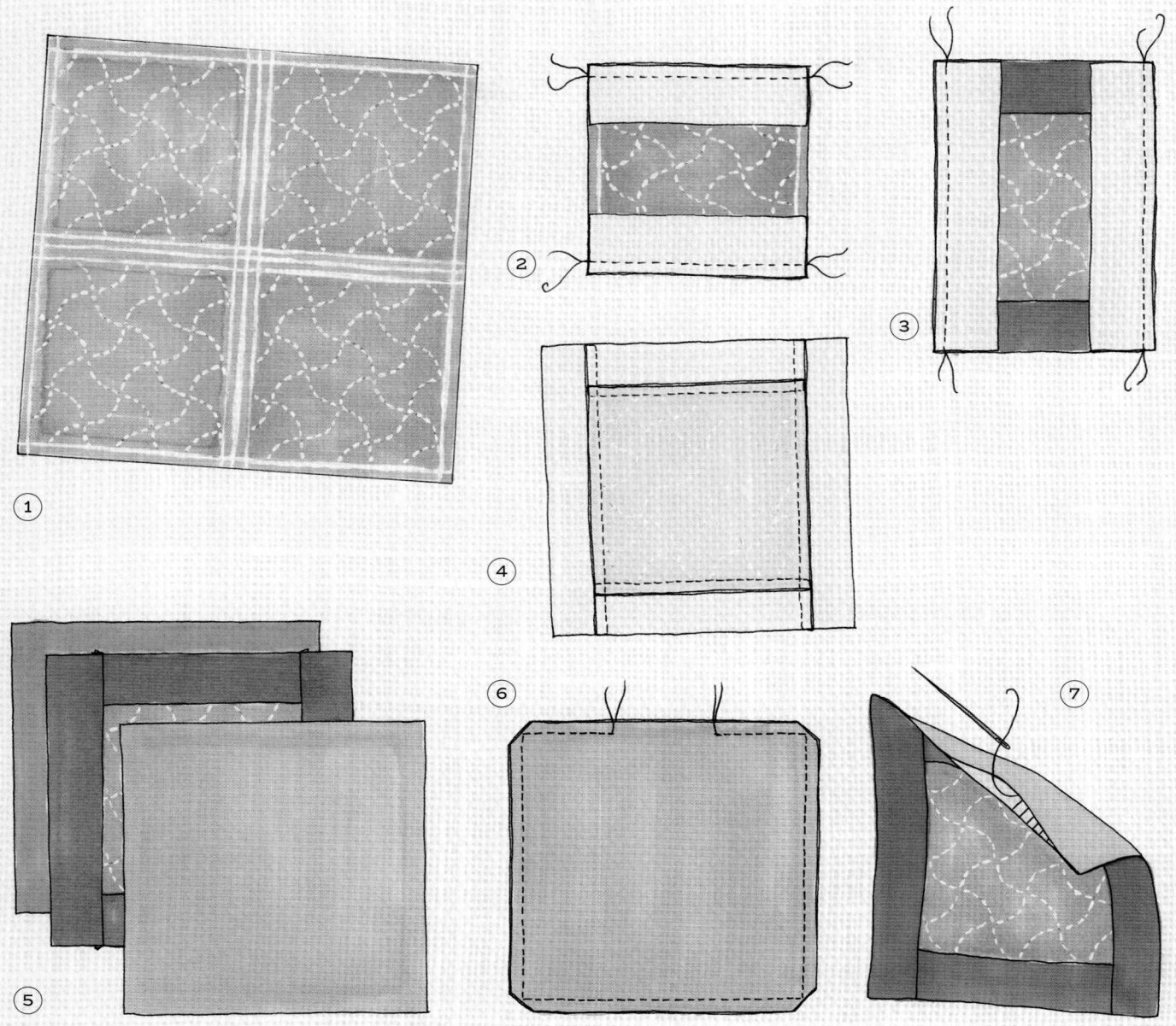

With right sides together, align two of the shorter, 1¼ x 5in (3.2 x 12.7cm), edging strips with the top and bottom edges of one coaster square. Machine stitch the edging strips to the coaster, ¼in (6mm) from the raw edges ②. Press the seams towards the outer edges.

With right sides together, align two of the longer, 1¼ x 6½in (3.2 x 16.5cm), edging strips with the sides of the coaster. Sew the edging strips to the coaster, ¼in (6mm) from the raw edges as before ③. Press the seams towards the edging strips ④.

Layer together a wadding square, the sashiko panel right side up, and finally the backing fabric wrong side up ⑤. Stitch the pieces together, ¼in (6mm) from the edges, leaving a 2in (5cm) gap for turning. Trim diagonally across the corners, taking care not to cut into the stitching ⑥.

Turn through, so the wadding is inside. Use a chopstick or knitting needle to push the corners out. Slipstitch the opening by hand (see page 21) ⑦ and press to finish.

Zabuton pincushion

YOU WILL NEED

- Pattern transferring equipment (see page 11)

- Sashiko fabric: 8½ x 8½in (21.5 x 21.5cm)

- Sashiko needle and thread

- Ribbon: ⅛ x 20in (3mm x 50.8cm)

- Fabric scissors

- Pins

- Backing fabric: 8½ x 8½in (21.5 x 21.5cm)

- Sewing machine/needle and thread

- Chopstick or knitting needle

- Iron

- Patterned fabric for inner pincushion: 6½ x 12½in (16.5 x 32cm)

- Wadding: small amount for inner pincushion

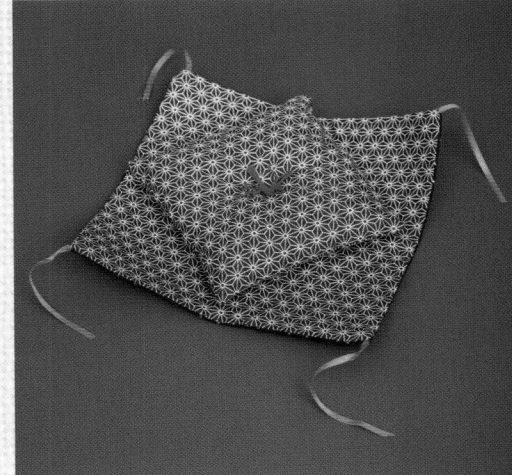

A zabuton floor cushion is an important part of any Japanese home, and is used as inspiration for this pincushion. For the sashiko pattern shown here, see page 120. Alternatively, select a different pattern from the Pattern Library (see pages 104–131) or design your own (see pages 14–15).

TIP
......

If you're designing your own pattern, draw it onto graph paper first, then fold the paper as shown for the fabric to be sure that it works well.

Traditional sashiko design shown here: SHIPPO TSUNAGI, also known as SEVEN TREASURES (see page 120).

Sashiko fabric – right side

Patterned fabric – right side

Patterned fabric – wrong side

Backing fabric – right side

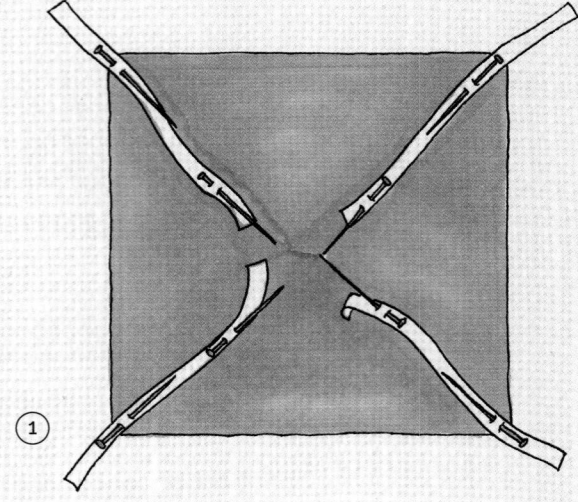

Transfer the design to your sashiko fabric (see pages 16–17), leaving a ¼in (6mm) seam allowance all round. Complete the stitching (see page 20). The four corners are the most important areas, so make sure they are as neat as possible.

Cut the ribbon into four equal-length pieces. Pin a ribbon to each corner of the sashiko, with the end overhanging the panel by up to 1in (2.5cm). Pin or tack the other ends of the ribbons to the fabric, to ensure they don't get caught up in the stitching ①.

Place the backing fabric on top of the sashiko panel, right sides together. Make sure the ribbons are still positioned exactly at each corner and the main length of ribbon is sandwiched between the layers. Sew a ¼in (6mm) seam allowance around, leaving a 2in (5cm) gap down one side to allow for turning through. Trim diagonally across the corners, taking care not to cut into the stitching. Turn through the gap, so the ribbons are on the outside.

Use a chopstick or knitting needle inside the panel to push the corners out as neatly as possible. Press the panel, then slipstitch (see page 21) the gap to close. Machine stitch close to the edges of the panel.

Fold the patterned fabric for the inner pincushion in half with right sides together and matching the short edges. Stitch the short edges together using a ½in (1.2cm) allowance. Leave a 2in (5cm) gap for turning.

Align the remaining edges with the seam positioned in the centre and press the seam open. Sew together the remaining two sides using a ¼in (6mm) seam allowance ②.

Trim diagonally across the corners, taking care not to cut into the stitching. Turn right side out and use a chopstick or knitting needle to push out the corners so they are sharp. Fill with the wadding until firm and slipstitch the gap to close.

Place the padded cushion, with the central seam facing down, onto the backing fabric of the sashiko panel ③. Using doubled sashiko thread, stitch from the top, through the centre of the pincushion and sashiko. Stitch back through to the top of the pincushion. Repeat with more thread and tightly tie the threads together to form a tassel in the centre. Trim the ends of the threads to neaten.

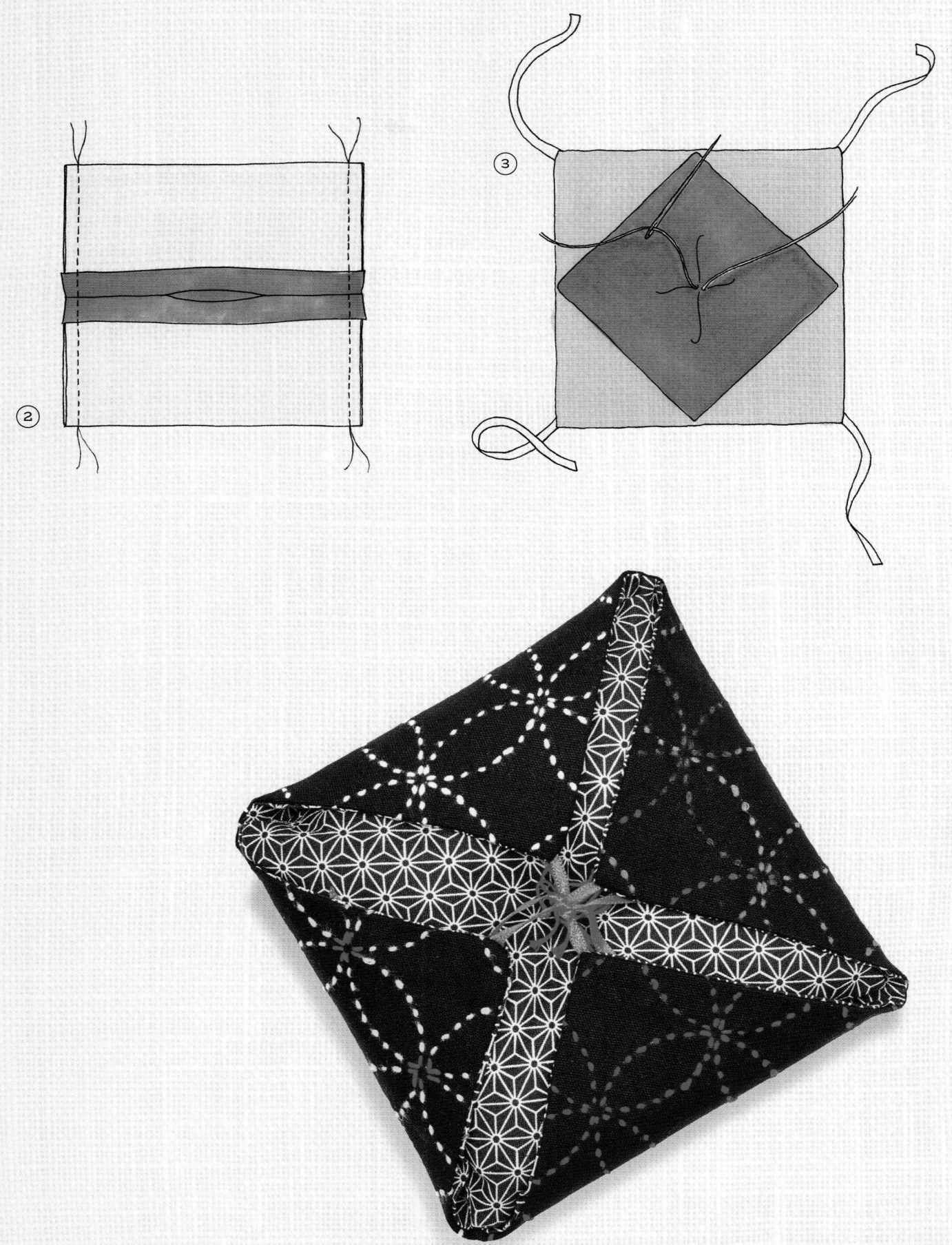

Needle case

YOU WILL NEED

- Tape measure and ruler
- Chalk pencil
- Pen and paper
- Pattern transferring equipment (see page 11)
- Sashiko fabric: 12 x 6in (30 x 15cm)
- Sashiko needle and thread
- Fusible wadding: 12 x 6in (30 x 15cm)
- Sewing machine/needle and thread
- Lining fabric: 1 piece, 12 x 6in (30 x 15cm); 1 piece, 12 x 4½in (30 x 11.5cm)
- Set of ⅛in (3mm) eyelets
- Sew-on press stud
- Fabric scissors
- Narrow ribbon: 24in (61cm) length
- 2 buttons (or one can be charm or large bead of your choice)

Sashiko design shown:
PLUM BLOSSOM (see page 107).

This little needle case has pockets to keep all of your sashiko equipment neat and tidy. An eyelet and ribbon are cleverly used to keep scissors or snips from getting lost.

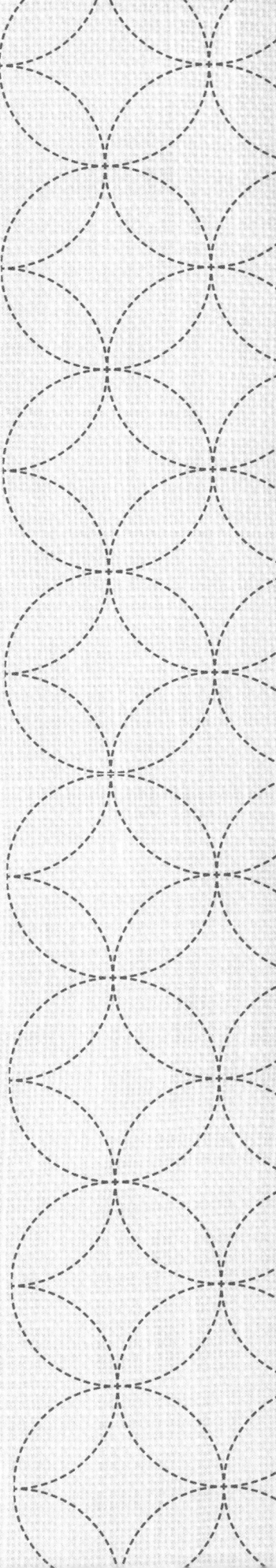

■ Sashiko fabric – right side

■ Lining fabric – right side

Draw a ¼in (6mm) border around the edge of your sashiko fabric with a chalk pencil. Draw a rectangle the same size on a piece of paper. Using the Plum Blossom template on page 107, trace the design onto the piece of paper. Alternatively, select a different design from the Pattern Library (see pages 104–131) or create your own (see pages 14–15). Transfer the design onto the fabric (see pages 16–17) ①. Complete the sashiko stitching (see page 20) inside the border.

Transfer a grid, positioned at an angle, onto the completed sashiko panel with a chalk pencil, using 1in (2.5cm) graph paper as a template (or photocopy the graph paper on page 134) ②. The grid can be drawn over the entire panel, even though you will only stitch it into the background, as the chalk washes away easily. Stitch the lines of the grid on the background only and not the flowers. The grid can be made larger or smaller, if preferred.

Place the sashiko panel, with right side facing up, on top of the wadding. Pin or tack the layers together to hold them in place.

To make the inside pocket, turn under and press a ¾in (2cm) hem on one long edge of the 12 x 4½in (30 x 11.5cm) lining piece. Stitch ¼in (6mm) from the pressed edge. With right side of pocket piece facing and the stitched hem at the top edge, mark two vertical lines 3½in (9cm) from each short

edge with a chalk pencil. Attach the eyelet, following the manufacturer's instructions, to the centre of the far right section of the pocket piece.

With the hem at the top of the pocket piece and aligning the raw edges, place the wrong side of the pocket piece on top of the right side of the 12 x 6in (30 x 15cm) lining fabric. To create the three pocket sections, stitch through both layers along the vertical chalk lines, continuing the stitching to the top edge of the larger lining piece ③.

Place the lining and sashiko panel right sides together. Stitch all the way around the edges, through all layers, using a ½in (1.2cm) seam allowance and leaving a 2in (5cm) gap for turning through. Trim diagonally across the corners, taking care not to cut into the stitching. Turn through, press and slipstitch the gap to close (see page 21).

Fold the needle case into three and mark the position of the button on the front flap, halfway down and 1in (2.5cm) in from the edge ④. The button is purely decorative. On the inside of the sewing case, stitch the ball part of the press stud, so it is in the same position as the button on the outside. Cover the ball of the press stud with chalk and fold the sewing case back into three, pressing the stud on to the fabric to mark the position of the socket part of the press stud. Sew the socket part in place.

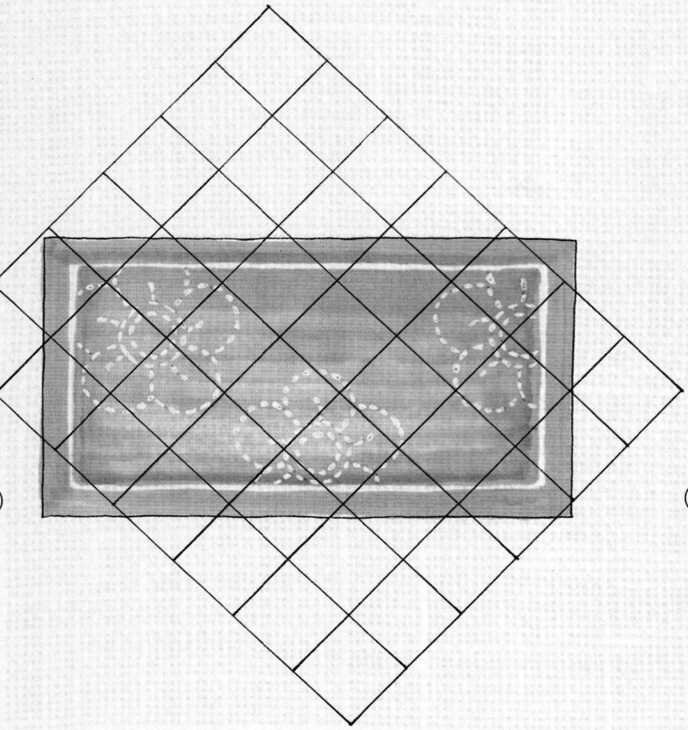

(2)

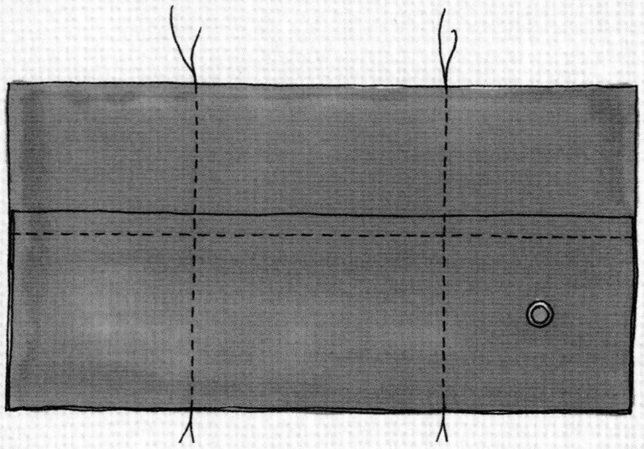

(3)

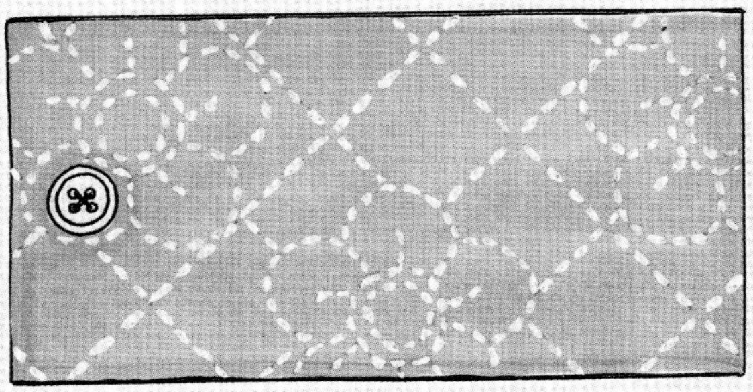

Fold the ribbon in half, wrap it around the top of a pair of scissors or snips, thread the ends of the ribbon through the loop, pulling them tight. Put the scissors in the far right pocket and thread the ends of the ribbon through the eyelet from the inside to the outside. Thread the ribbon through the button, or you can use a bead or charm, and tie into a knot.

Now when you need to use your scissors or snips you simply pull them out of the pocket. To prevent you from losing them the button or charm will be blocked by the eyelet. Also, to put them back in the pocket, simply pull the charm.

(4)

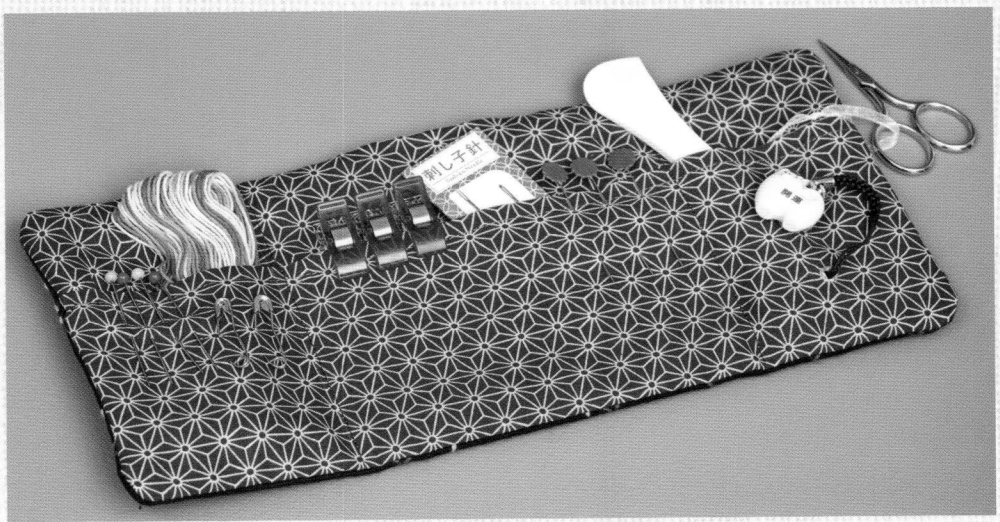

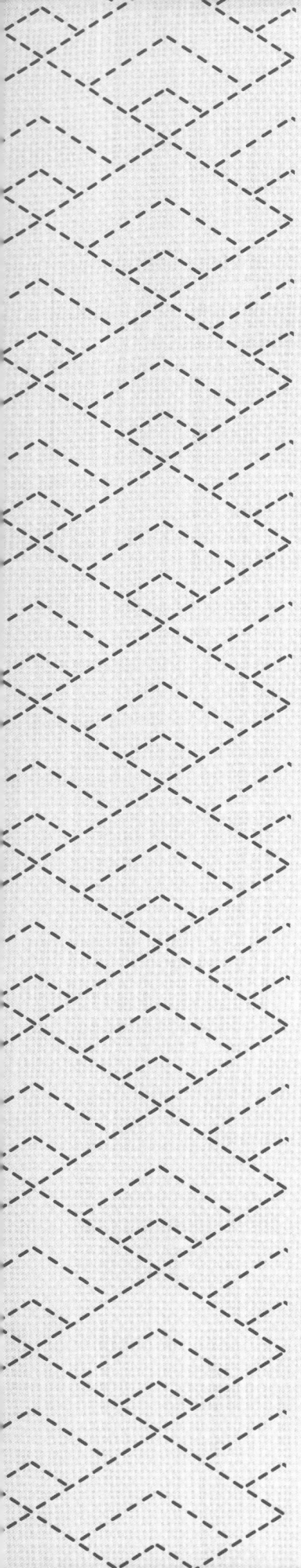

Book cover

YOU WILL NEED

- Sashiko fabric: 14 x 9½in (35.6 x 24cm), pre-printed Hitomezashi fabric or plain fabric to draw onto

- Medium-weight iron-on interfacing: 14 x 9½in (35.6 x 24cm)

- Graph paper (optional)

- Fabric marker

- Iron

- Sashiko needle and thread

- Plain fabric: 5 x 9½in (12.5 x 24cm) plain fabric

- Lining fabric: 17 x 9½in (43 x 24cm)

- Sewing machine/needle and thread

- A5 or half letter-size book to be covered

This type of sashiko is called Hitomezashi or one-stitch sashiko. If you stick to regular book sizes, the cover can easily be reused.

- Sashiko fabric – right side
- Sashiko fabric – wrong side
- Plain fabric – wrong side
- Lining fabric – right side

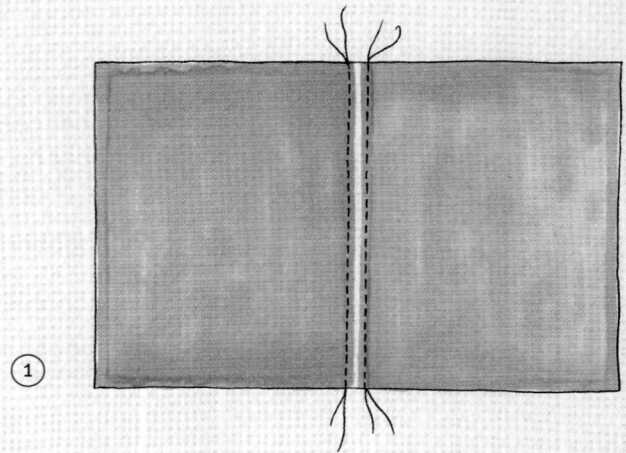

If you aren't using pre-printed fabric, place the interfacing over graph paper and mark on equally spaced dots to fill the fabric. This method works perfectly well, as the stitch length is the same on both the back and the front. This differs from the traditional sashiko stitch ratio and is specific to Hitomezashi fabric. You can make these dots as close together or as far apart as you want. The design shown has three stitches to an inch (2.5cm).

Iron the interfacing to the reverse of your main fabric and begin stitching (see page 20). If you wish to match the design shown here, see page 106 for the template. However, there are lots of possibilities, so you can experiment with the stitches: you don't always have to stitch equal lines; you can use alternative spacing for your base stitches; you can divide the fabric into strips of different patterns; or you can stitch assorted blocks.

If you're using pre-printed fabric, iron on the interfacing once you have stitched the design.

Mark a vertical line down the centre of the sashiko panel. Using a very small running stitch, with a sewing machine or by hand, sew a line of stitching ¼in (6mm) from each side of the marked line ①. By making the stitches as small as possible, you will be able to catch in all of the threads and then cut the fabric into two equal sections.

With rights sides together, stitch the long edges of the plain centre panel to each sashiko piece, using a neat running stitch, by hand or machine, and allowing a ½in (1.2cm) seam ②. Press the seams towards the centre panel.

Place the book cover front and the lining fabric right sides together and stitch around the edges using a ¼in (6mm) seam allowance and leaving a 2in (5cm) gap to turn through. Turn through and press. Slipstitch the gap to close (see page 21).

Lay your book open on the centre of the book cover lining and fold the short sides of the sashiko cover to the inside of the front and back cover of the book. Make sure the book closes and the cover is not too tight before you slipstitch the tops of the folded edges to the fabric cover ③.

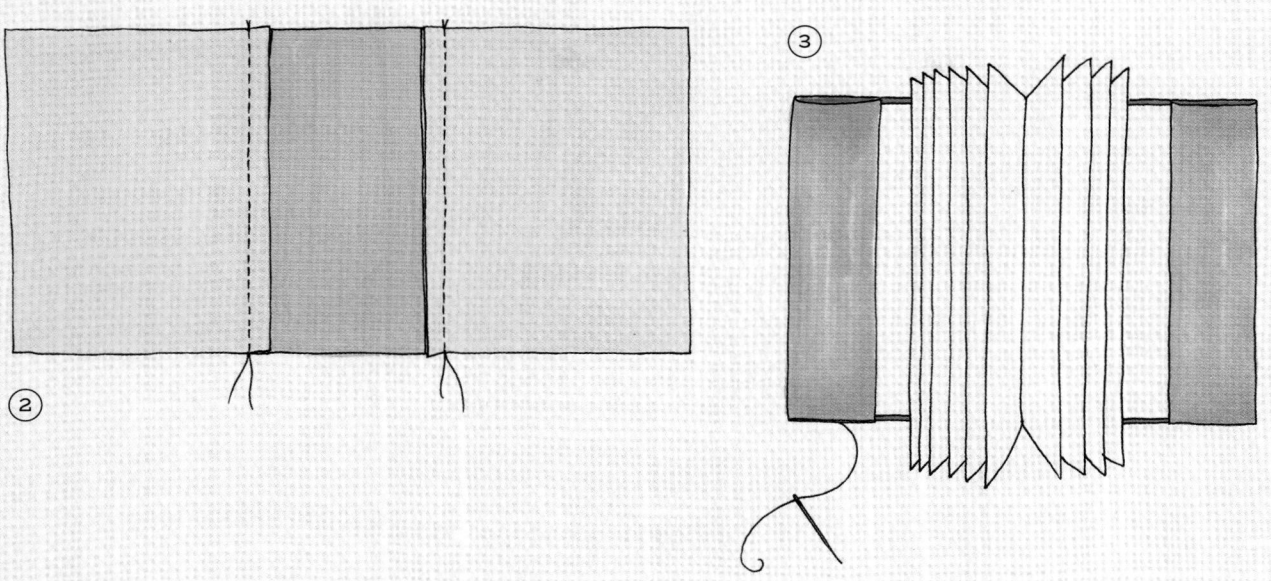

Kinchaku craft bag

YOU WILL NEED

- Pattern transferring equipment (see page 11)
- Sashiko fabric: 5 pieces, 9 x 9in (23 x 23cm)
- Wadding: 5 pieces, each slightly larger than your fabric
- Thin backing fabric: 5 pieces, 9 x 9in (23 x 23cm)
- Pins
- Sashiko needle and thread
- Lining fabric: 5 pieces, 9 x 9in (23 x 23cm)
- Sewing needle and thread
- Iron
- Drawstring loop fabric, such as the lining fabric: 12 pieces, 4 x 3in (10 x 7.5cm)
- Cord: 2 pieces, 36in (90cm) long
- Bead: $5/8$–$3/4$in (1.5–2cm) wide with $1/4$in (6mm) hole

Kinchaku simply means 'purse'. The beauty of the kinchaku style is that when opened it makes for a very large topped bag.

You can stitch as many sides of this bag as you want. On two sides I designed my own patterns by starting off with a grid (see pages 14–15) and simply experimenting by adding lines until I was happy with it. The other sides are based on a basketweave design.

TIP
......

This bag makes a great storage box if made with a large piece of fabric and heavyweight stiffener.

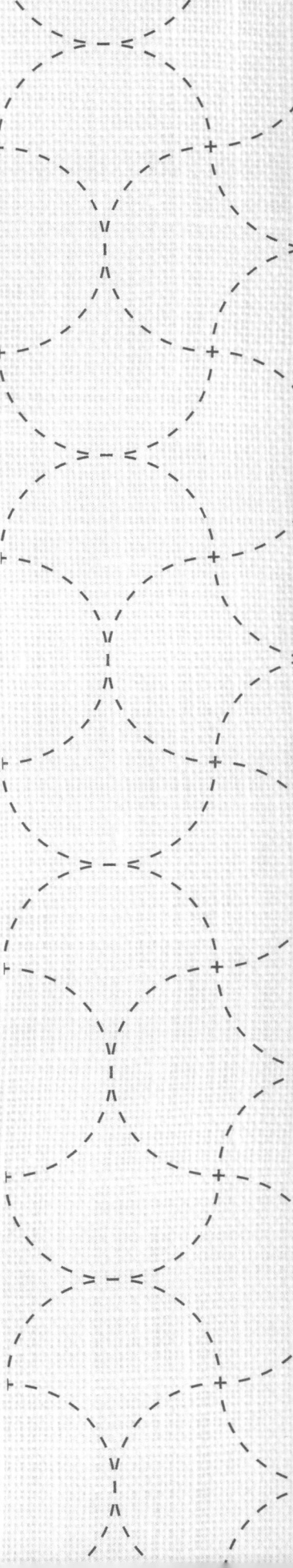

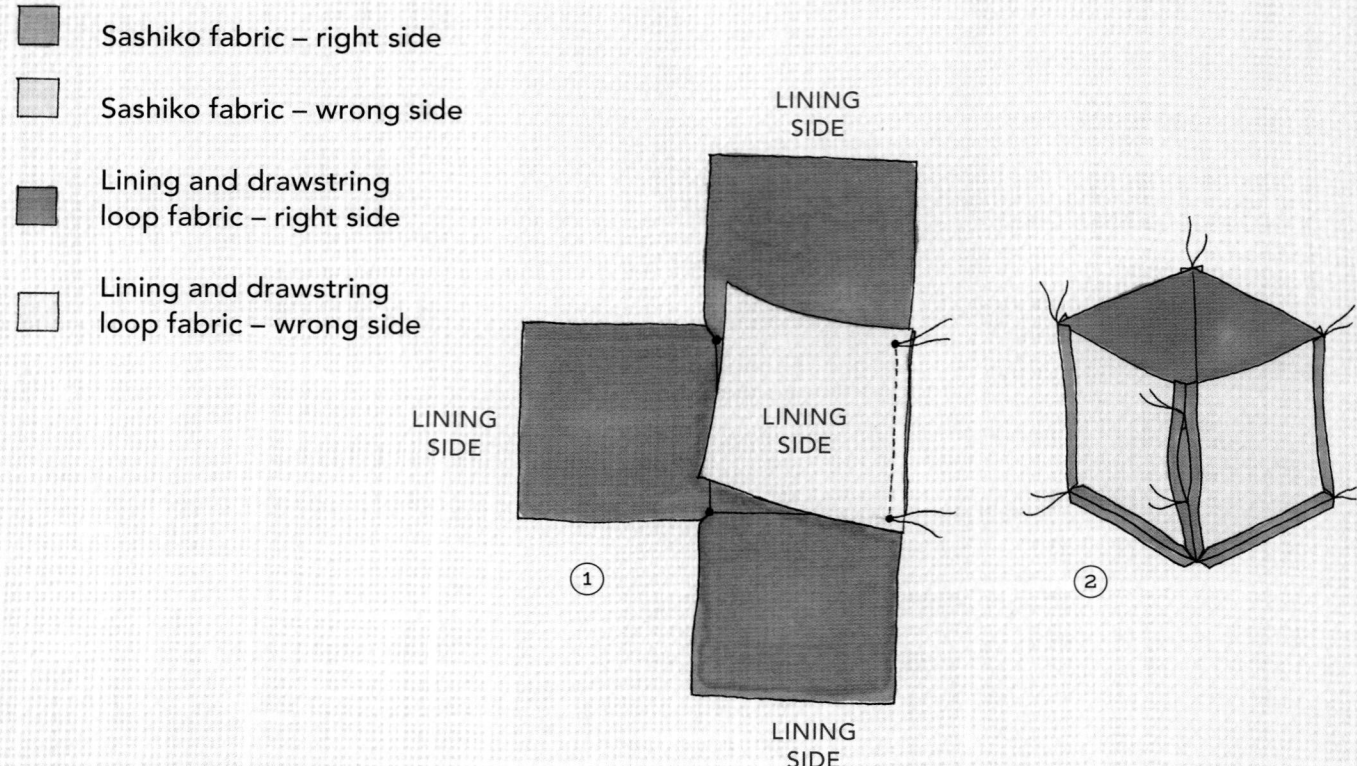

- ■ Sashiko fabric – right side
- □ Sashiko fabric – wrong side
- ■ Lining and drawstring loop fabric – right side
- □ Lining and drawstring loop fabric – wrong side

LINING SIDE

LINING SIDE

LINING SIDE

LINING SIDE

① ②

Select your sashiko designs from the Pattern Library (see pages 104–131) or create your own (see page 14–15). Transfer your designs onto the sashiko fabric pieces (see pages 16–17).

Layer the sashiko fabric, wadding and thin backing fabric together for each of the five squares. Pin or tack these pieces together. Complete the sashiko, stitching through all layers (see page 20). To make up the lining, mark a dot at the ⅜in (1cm) seam allowance on each corner of the bag base and the lower edges of the side pieces. With right sides together, sew the four side pieces to each edge of the base, stitching between the dots ①.

Sew the side seams to form a box shape ② using a ⅜in (1cm) seam allowance, sewing from the top of the bag lining to the dot at the base, and leaving a 5in (12.5cm) gap on one side for turning through later. Cut across the corners, taking care not to cut into the stitching. Press the seams open.

Now make the loops for the drawstring. Fold one of the drawstring loop pieces in half lengthways and press ③.

Open it up and fold each side into the centre ④. Press in half again and sew down each side of the strip ⑤.

Repeat with the other 11 strips. Fold each strip in half to form a loop ⑥.

Put together your sashiko panels in the same way as you did the lining squares but without leaving a turning gap. With your sashiko panels right side out, pin three loops to the top of each side as shown, with the raw edges facing up and aligning with the top of the bag ⑦.

Turn your liner so that the wrong side is outside and place your sashiko panel inside the liner ⑧. Spend some time lining everything up neatly and pin together. The loops will

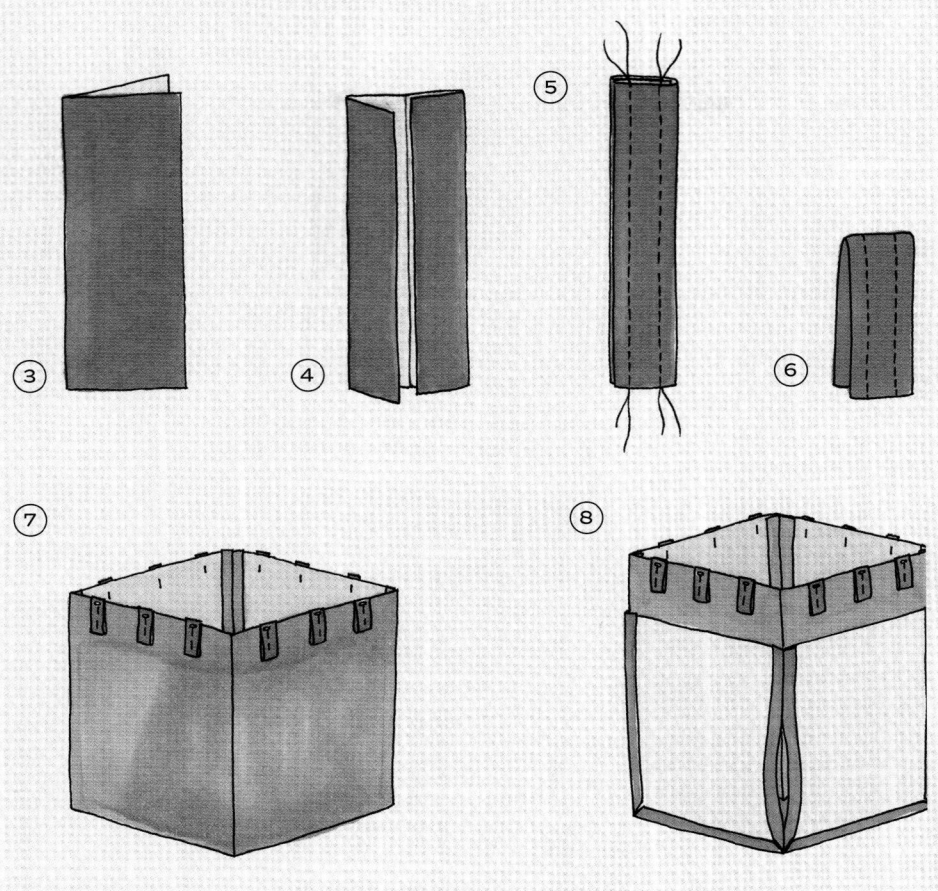

be sandwiched between the sashiko panels and the liner. This will mean that they are neatly secured between the layers when it is turned right side out.

Stitch a ⅜in (1cm) seam around the top of your bag ⑨. Make sure to check that the loops are still in place. Turn the bag through the gap you left in the liner. Slipstitch (see page 21) the turning gap in the lining closed ⑩.

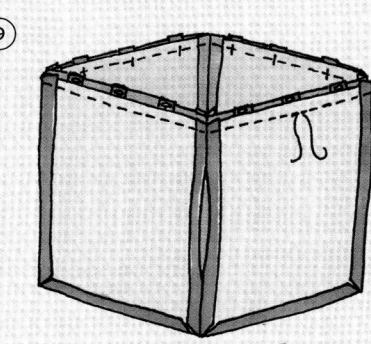

Thread the cord through the loops. Push both ends of the cord through a large bead and tie a knot to secure it. If you don't have a bead, just tie a knot in the cord.

Cushion cover

YOU WILL NEED

- Sashiko fabric:
  17 x 17in (43 x 43cm)

- Tailor's chalk,
  or other fabric marker

- Pen and paper

- Scissors

- Pins

- Pattern transferring equipment
  (see page 11)

- Fabric for circular panel:
  8 x 8in (20 x 20cm)

- Featherweight fusible interfacing:
  8 x 8in (20 x 20cm)

- Iron

- Sewing machine/needle
  and thread

- Fabric scissors

- Fabric for reverse of cushion:
  17 x 17in (43 x 43cm)

- 17in (43cm) square of white
  lightweight or non-woven
  interfacing (optional, for
  transferring the design)

- 16 x 16in (40 x 40cm) square
  cushion form

TIP

......

To make the cushion
stronger, you can
iron on the interfacing
to the back of the
sashiko panel. This is
optional, but gives a
better finish.

Sashiko design shown:
HISHI SEIGAIHA (see page 116).

- Sashiko fabric – right side
- Circular panel – right side
- Circular panel – wrong side
- Backing fabric – wrong side
- Interfacing

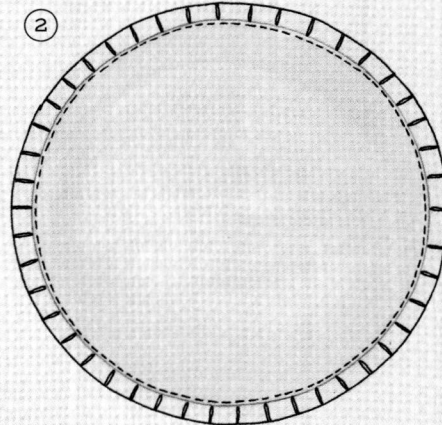

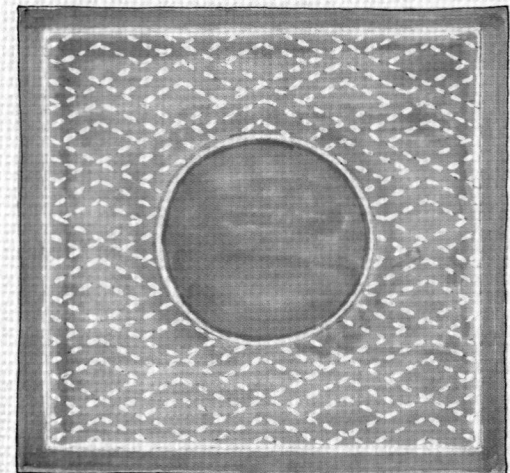

Enlarge the template on page 107 to 8in (20cm) and cut it out. Mark the centre of the sashiko fabric with tailor's chalk. Pin the circular template to the centre of the fabric, using the mark as a reference. Draw around the circle with chalk.

For the sashiko pattern shown here, use the pattern on page 116. Alternatively, you can select a different pattern from the Pattern Library (see pages 104–131) or design your own (see pages 14–15). Transfer the pattern to the fabric (see pages 16–17), leaving the circular area empty. This will be used later for the appliqué panel. Complete the sashiko stitching (see page 20), leaving a ¼in (6mm) seam allowance around the edge of the fabric. ①.

Place the circular template on the 7³⁄₃₂in (18cm) square of fabric and cut out the fabric. Following the inner line on the template, trim the template to a 6¹¹⁄₁₆in (19cm) diameter circle. Use this template to cut out a circle from the featherweight interfacing. Iron the interfacing onto the centre of the wrong side of the larger circle of fabric. Machine stitch around the circle, just inside the edge of the interfacing. This makes a much neater panel. Snip around the edges of the circle ②. Press the edges in to neaten.

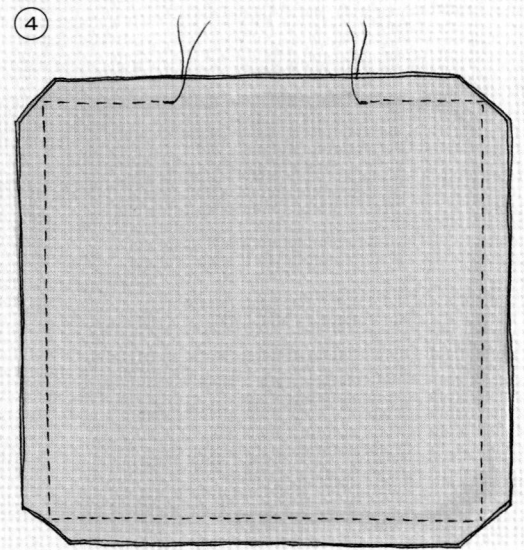

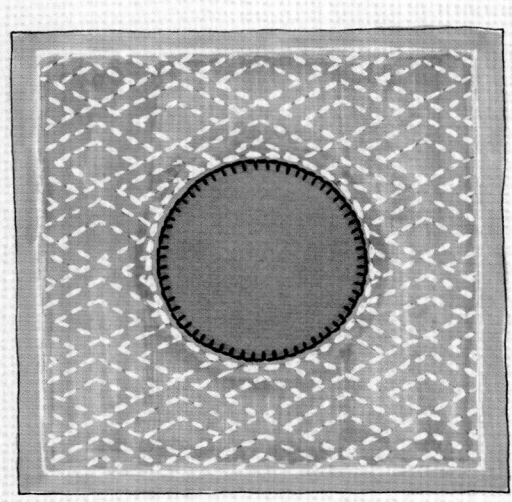

Place the fabric circle onto the right side of the cushion front and use an appliqué stitch (see page 21) to sew it down. You will have a gap between the fabric circle and the sashiko stitching on the cushion front. Stitch a single line of sashiko stitches around the edge of the empty circular area ③.

Place the sashiko panel and the fabric for the reverse of the cushion right sides together and machine stitch a ½in (1.2cm) seam all around the edges to join the pieces, leaving a 6in (15cm) gap in one side. Cut diagonally into the corners, taking care not to cut into the stitching ④.

Turn through and insert the cushion pad through the gap. Neatly slipstitch (see page 21) the gap closed.

Wall hanging

- Sashiko fabric: 19 x 15in (48.3 x 38cm)

- Sashiko needle and thread

- Featherweight interfacing: 19 x 15in (48.3 x 38cm)

- Iron

- Sewing needle and thread

- Pins

- Brocade: 2 pieces, 19 x 3in (48.3 x 7.5cm); 2 pieces, 19 x 6in (48.3 x 15cm); 1 piece, 14 x 8in (35.6 x 20cm): cut in half to make 2 pieces, 14 x 4in (35.6 x 10cm) for the Futai

- Complementary fabric: 1 piece, 19 x 15in (48.3 x 38cm); 1 piece, 19 x 12in (48.3 x 30.5cm)

- Pattern transferring equipment (see page 11)

In some Japanese inns and houses you will find an alcove set into the wall. These are called Tokonoma. They are usually in the reception room and are places to display an Ikebana flower arrangement or a special scroll, known as Kakejiku, as a welcome to the home. This is a version of a welcome scroll.

- Chopstick or knitting needle

- Backing fabric: the same size as finished wall hanging (for accuracy, cut once your front panel is complete)

- Dowel or bamboo: 25in (63cm) length

- Cord for hanger: 59in (150cm) of $^5/_{16}$in (8mm) braided cord

TIP
......

Here, silk brocade from Kyoto, Japan, has been used, but any fabric can be substituted for the brocade.

Sashiko design shown: BAMBOO (see page 108).

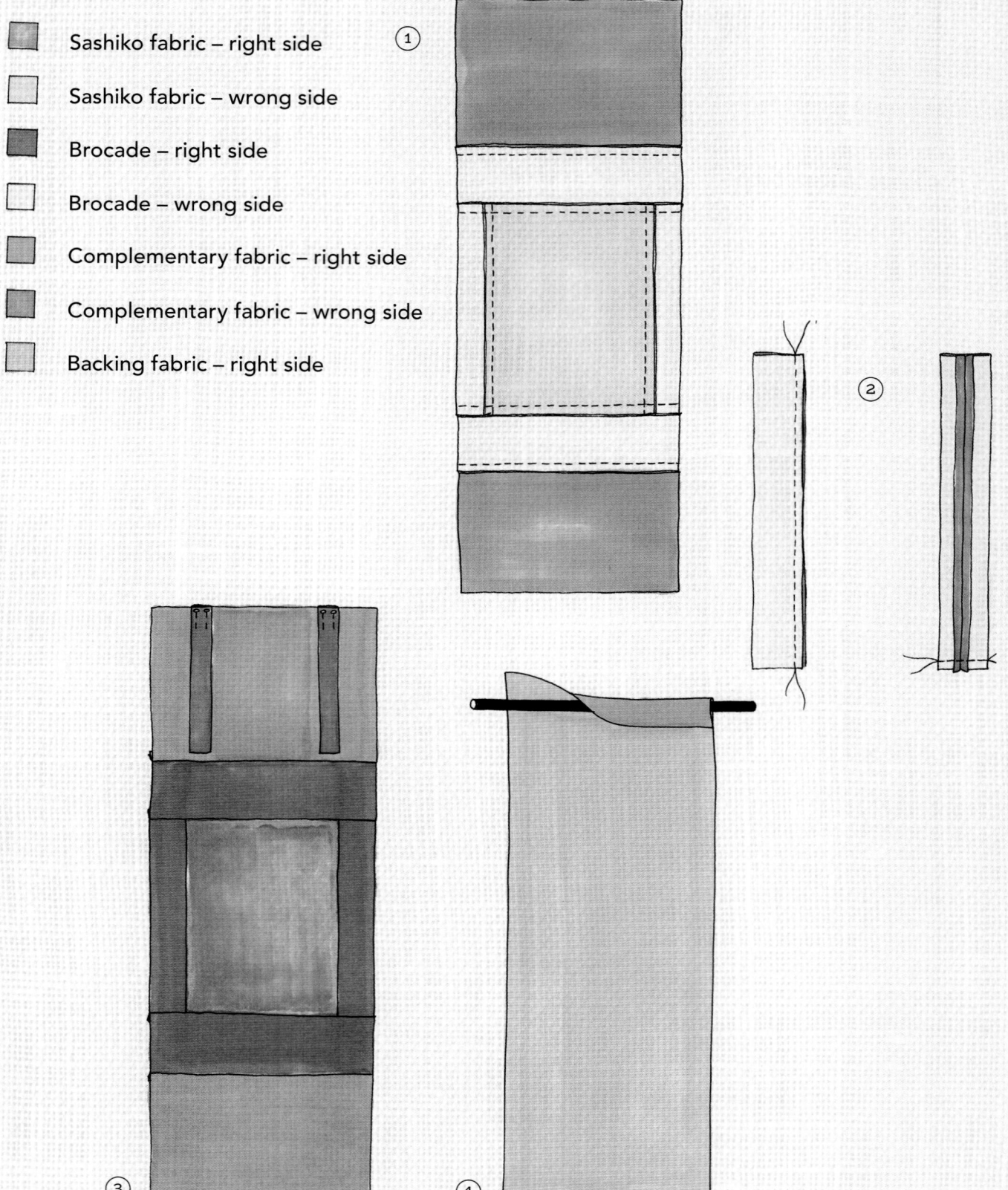

- Sashiko fabric – right side
- Sashiko fabric – wrong side
- Brocade – right side
- Brocade – wrong side
- Complementary fabric – right side
- Complementary fabric – wrong side
- Backing fabric – right side

For the sashiko pattern shown here, use the template provided on page 108. Alternatively, you can select a different pattern from the Pattern Library (see pages 104–131) or design your own (see pages 14–15). Transfer the pattern to the sashiko fabric (see pages 16–17) and complete the stitching (see page 20).

To add strength to the sashiko, you can iron on featherweight interfacing (here it is added so that the sashiko is a similar weight to the silk brocade). Lay out all the pieces of fabric as shown.

With right sides together, sew the 19 x 3in (48.3 x 7.5cm) brocade strips to the sashiko panel, using a ½in (1.2cm) seam allowance. Press after each strip has been added. With right sides together, sew the larger brocade strips to the top and bottom of the sashiko panel.

With right sides together, sew the longer complementary coloured fabric piece to the top and the shorter piece to the bottom of the panel. (1). This completes the front panel.

On a traditional Kakejiku there are also two strips of fabric that are attached to the top of the hanging. These are called Futai. Originally they were used to scare birds away from landing on the scrolls when hung outside. Here they are made with two strips of brocade. Simply fold each piece of brocade in half lengthways and stitch down the long side, using a ¼in (6mm) seam allowance. Move the seam to the back and press flat. Stitch along one short edge, using a ¼in (6mm) seam allowance (2). Use a chopstick or knitting needle to turn through to the right side and press.

The top fabric panel is longer than the bottom to allow for the channel that holds the dowel or bamboo. With right sides together, align the raw edges of the Futai with the top of the front panel, positioning them just inside the brocade edging (3). Pin in place. Cut the backing fabric to the same size as the front panel and, with right sides together, sew together the two pieces around all sides, using a ½in (1.2cm) seam allowance and leaving a 4in (10cm) gap on the top edge. Trim diagonally across the corners, taking care not to cut into the stitching. Turn through and use a chopstick or knitting needle to push out the corners. Press carefully. Slipstitch (see page 21) the gap to close.

Lay the dowel on the back of the hanging. Fold the hanging over until it covers the dowel plus 1in (2.5cm) (4). Pin in place and remove the dowel. Pin down the Futai and run a neat line of stitches straight across. Insert the dowel into the channel.

Tie the hanging cord onto each side of the dowel with a simple knot or bow.

Table runner

YOU WILL NEED

- Complementary fabrics in plain or patterned designs: 5 pieces, 4 x 4in (10 x 10cm); 10 pieces, 4 x 6in (10 x 15cm); 5 pieces, 6 x 6in (15 x 15cm)

  For a longer runner, cut 1 piece each of 4 x 4in (10 x 10cm) and 6 x 6in (15 x 15cm), and 2 pieces of 4 x 6in (10 x 15cm) for each extra block

- Sewing needle and thread

- Iron

- Backing fabric: 13¾ x 46¾in (35 x 119cm)

  For a longer runner, add an extra 8½in (21.5cm) to the length of the longer border pieces for each additional block

- Featherweight interfacing: 9 x 43¼in (23 x 110cm)

- Permanent pen or pencil

- Pattern transferring equipment (see page 11)

- Border fabric in complementary colour: 2 pieces, 2½ x 9in (7.5 x 23cm); 2 pieces, 3 x 46¾in (75 x 119cm) for a five-block runner. Add an extra 8½in (21.5cm) to the length of the longer border pieces for each additional block

- Chopstick or knitting needle

- ■ Fabric A – right side
- □ Fabric A – wrong side
- ■ Fabric B – right side
- □ Fabric B – wrong side
- ■ Fabric C – right side
- □ Fabric C – wrong side
- ■ Fabric D – right side
- □ Fabric D – wrong side
- □ Interfacing

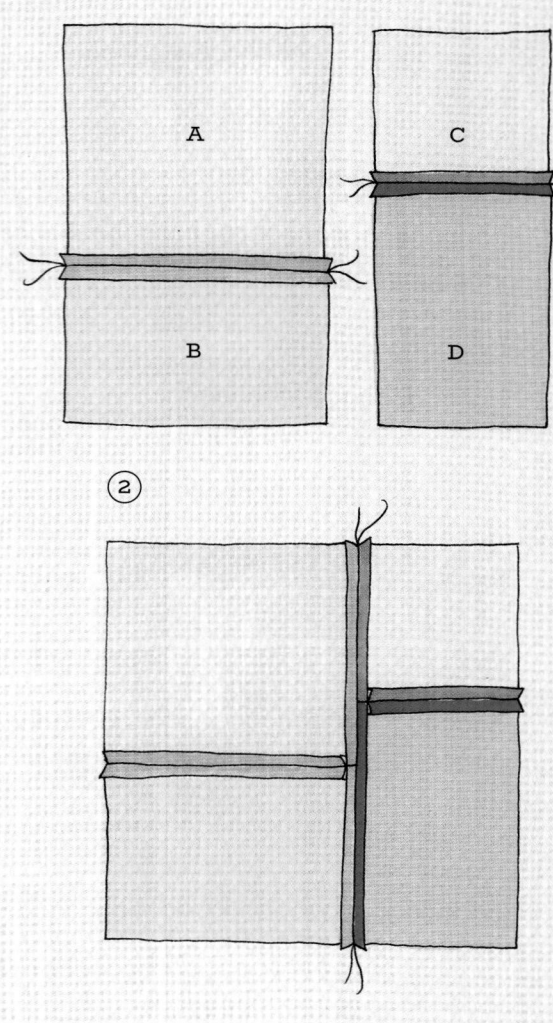

Arrange your fabrics to form five multi-patterned blocks of four patchwork pieces, varying the layout ①.

With each block, sew together A and B, then C and D, using ³⁄₈in (1cm) seam allowances. Next, sew the two together to form a square, using a ³⁄₈in (1cm) seam allowance ②. Each block should be the same size when all four pieces are sewn together. Press all the seams flat on the reverse.

Sew each block together to form a strip, using a ³⁄₈in (1cm) seam allowance.

Cut the featherweight interfacing to the same size as the finished strip of blocks. Using a permanent pen or pencil, draw a grid onto the interfacing ③.

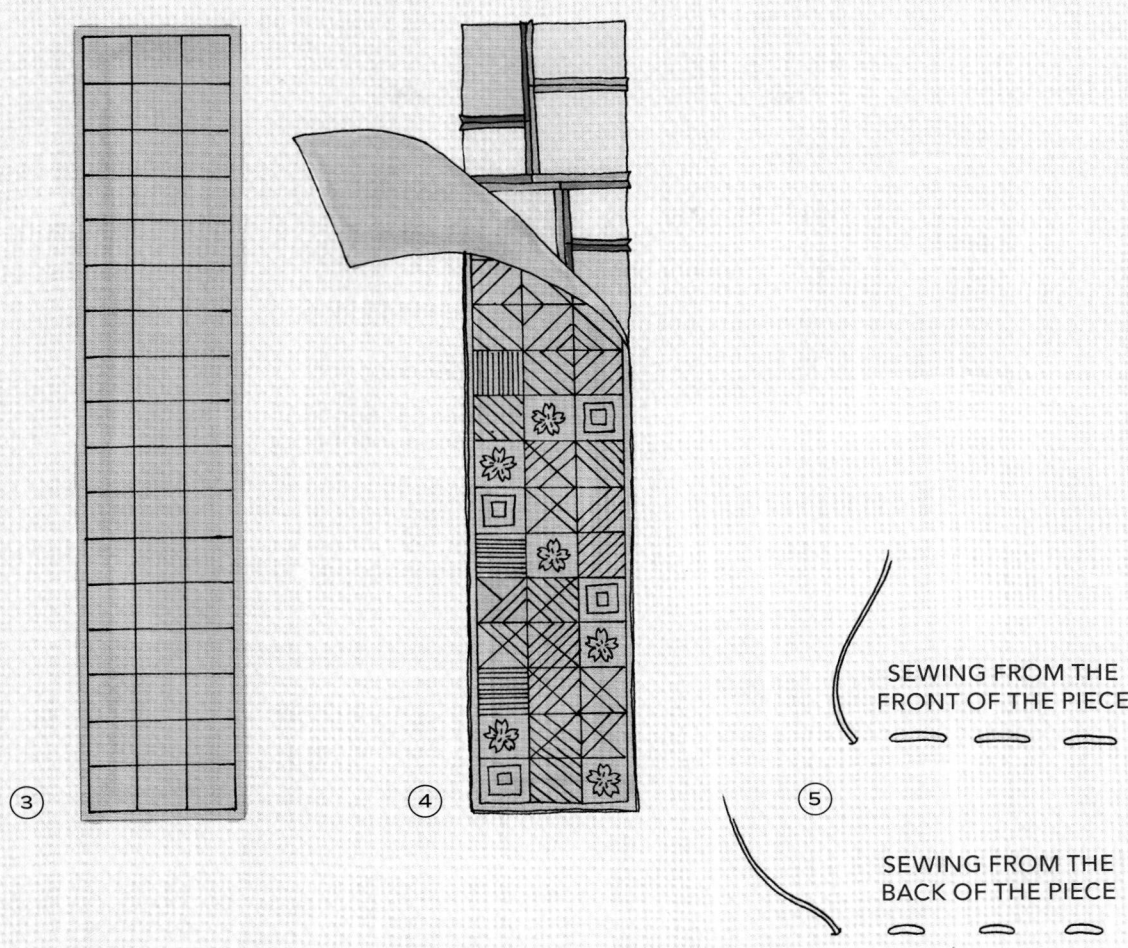

③　④　⑤

SEWING FROM THE
FRONT OF THE PIECE

SEWING FROM THE
BACK OF THE PIECE

Trace or draw a pattern into each square. Select patterns from the Pattern Library (see pages 104–131) or design your own (see pages 14–15). There is a template for the flower shown here on page 108. Transfer the designs to the squares (see pages 16–17).

Once you have drawn your designs, place the featherweight interfacing on the reverse of your strip of blocks and iron it on, making sure the panel doesn't distort as you iron it ④.

Because you are stitching from the back of the work, following the lines on the interfacing, you will need to adjust the stitch length. When sewing from the front, you would use a longer stitch, then a short space in between. Because you are working from the back, you need to reverse this ⑤.

Complete the stitching in your chosen designs and colours (see page 20). With right sides together, sew the short border pieces to each end of the strip of blocks. Press the seams open.

With right sides together, stitch the long border pieces to each side of the strip of blocks. Press the seams open.

With right sides together, sew the backing to the runner, stitching a ⅜in (1cm) seam all around and leaving a 4in (10cm) gap to turn through. Use a chopstick or knitting needle to poke out the corners. Press and slipstitch (see page 21) the gap to close. To finish, stitch neatly around the edge in the ditch between the centre panel and border of the table runner. This can be sashiko by hand, or with a sewing machine.

Laundry bag

YOU WILL NEED

- Pre-printed sashiko fabric (only a section of the design will be used) or plain sashiko fabric: 44 x 15in (112 x 38cm)

- Sashiko needle and thread

- Contrasting fabric for the top of the bag: 2½ x 15in (6.25 x 38cm), cut in half lengthways

- Main fabric pieces for drawstring loops: 8 pieces, 3 x 4in (7.5 x 10cm)

- Lining fabric of your choice: 47 x 15in (119.5 x 38cm)

- Pattern transferring equipment (see page 11)

- Chaco paper

- Twisted cord: 1¼yd (1.1m) length of ¼in (6mm) wide cord

- Sewing machine/needle and thread

Sashiko design shown: ASANOHA (see page 109).

TIP
......

This bag can be used for many things, not just laundry. It could be a baby changing bag, peg bag or, if you added a waterproof lining, it would make an ideal swimming bag.

- ☐ Sashiko fabric – right side
- ▨ Sashiko fabric – wrong side
- ▦ Contrasting fabric – right side
- ☐ Contrasting fabric – wrong side
- ▪ Lining fabric – right side
- ☐ Lining fabric – wrong side

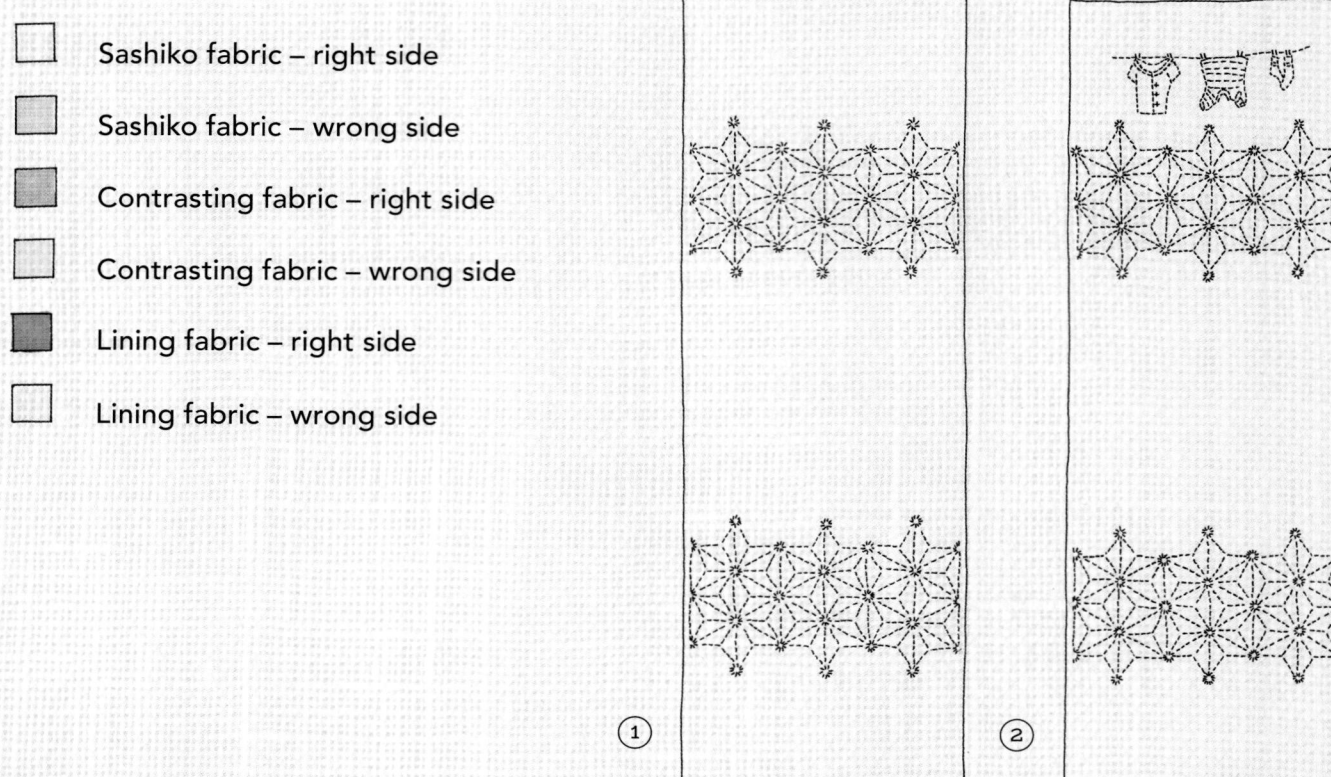

The beauty of pre-printed fabric is that you can use as much or as little of the design as you want. Here I've chosen to use a strip of the design and then, after washing away the pre-printed design, If you cannot get hold of pre-printed sashiko fabric, you can use plain sashiko fabric and the template on page 109. Alternatively, you can select a different pattern from the Pattern Library (see pages 104–131) or design your own (see pages 14–15). Transfer your chosen design to the fabric (see pages 16–17).

You can stitch as much as you want; I wanted a classic-looking laundry bag, so I stitched the design towards the bottom end of the bag only. I repeated this on the reverse side ①. Once the stitching is complete, you will need to wash away the remaining unused pattern. Note that pre-printed lines on light fabric will take longer to disappear.

For the front of the laundry bag I chose to add a selection of clothing designs (see page 109 for the template). Choose as many as you want or add others. If the bag is for a baby, for example, baby grows would be great, or a swimming costume for a swimming bag. Transfer or draw the clothes onto a sheet of plain paper and try out different placements until you are happy. Then, draw a line across the top of them to form the washing line and add a couple of stitches on each item to look like clothes pegs. Transfer the finished washing line design to your sashiko fabric using the Chaco paper method (see page 16). Stitch on your design (see page 20) ②.

With right sides together, stitch a strip of the contrasting fabric to each end of your finished sashiko panel, using a ½in (1.2cm) seam allowance ③. Press the seams open.

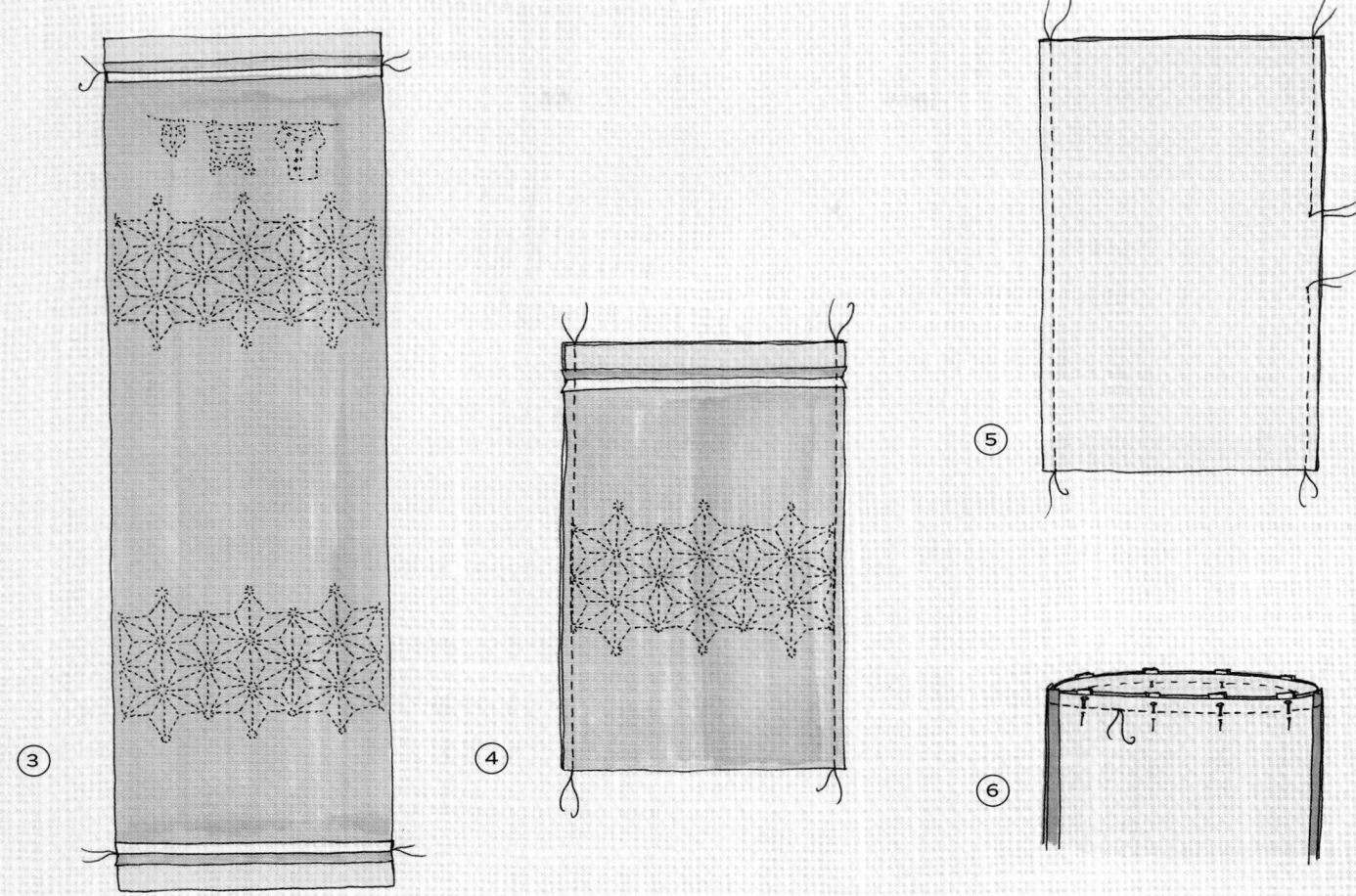

Fold the fabric in half, with right sides together and matching the contrasting strips at the top. Stitch a ½in (1.2cm) seam down each side ④.

Fold the lining fabric in half, so it is the same size as the sashiko panel. Sew up the sides only, but leave a 4in (10cm) gap on one of the sides for turning through later ⑤.

You now need to make the loops for your drawstring and put the bag together. This is exactly the same as making the loops for the kinchaku bag (see page 46). Pin four loops on the right side of each side of the sashiko bag.

Place your outer sashiko bag inside the liner. Make sure that both the bag and the liner are right sides together before you pin around the top and sew a ½in (1.2cm) hem right around the top of your bag ⑥.

Turn the bag through the gap you left in the liner. Slipstitch (see page 21) the gap to finish.

To give the bag a professional finish, put a neat row of stitches around the top of your bag either by hand or on your sewing machine.

Thread the cord through the loops and tie the ends in a knot.

Sashiko design shown:
SHIPPO TSUNAGI (see page 120).

Japanese-bound book

YOU WILL NEED

- Sashiko fabric: 9 x 12½in (23 x 31.8cm)

- Sashiko needle and thread

- Paper, 8¼ x 12in (21 x 29.7cm) such as watercolour or copier paper: 20 sheets, folded in half

- Medium-weight paper: 6 x 8½in (14.8 x 21.6cm), for template

- Pattern transferring equipment (see page 11)

- Four sets of ⅛in (3mm) eyelets

- Small hammer or eyelet setting tool

- Strong cord, such as linen bookbinding cord, or jewellery-making cord: 33in (84cm long)

- Tapestry needle

- Iron

- Medium-weight stiffener or interfacing: 9 x 12½in (23 x 31.8cm)

- Card: 2 pieces, 6 x 8½in (14.8 x 21.6cm)

- 2 bulldog clips

- Screw punch, bradawl or snip

TIP
......

At some point, you may want to use the cover for another book. If so, simply clip the pages together on the open edge and unstring. Pop a cardboard cover on the front and restring.

NOTE: The instructions are for an approximately A5 or half letter-size book.

◻ Interfacing

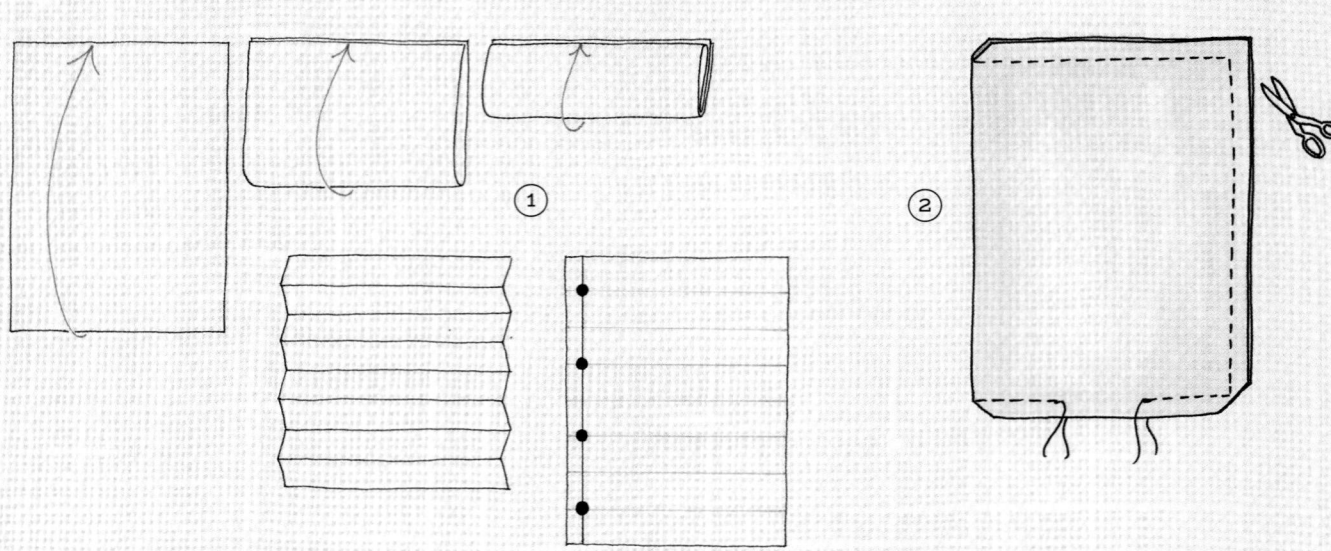

Take the medium-weight sheet of paper and fold it in half widthways three times. This will give you a template with eight sections. Draw a line ½in (1.5cm) in from the edge of the paper. Make four marks to indicate where holes will be punched ①. Place the folded paper on top of the inner papers and use a screw punch or bradawl to punch through the inner papers. Repeat with both pieces of card for the cover.

Prepare the sashiko front cover. If you have pre-printed sashiko fabric, you can fill in some of the stitching and add another sashiko design to the area left unstitched, as has been done here. For the sashiko pattern used here, see page 120. Alternatively, you can select a different pattern from the Pattern Library (see pages 104–131) or design your own (see pages 14–15). Transfer your chosen patterns onto the fabric (see pages 16–17). Complete the sashiko stitching (see page 20).

Iron the stiffener/interfacing onto the back of the fabric. Fold in half, with wrong sides together. Sew a ¼in (6mm) seam around the edge, leaving a gap of approximately 2in (5cm) to turn the fabric through. Trim off the corners to make a neater edge when turned through ②. Slipstitch (see page 21) the gap neatly.

Using the template, mark the hole spacings onto the sashiko front with chalk or an erasable marking pen. Make a small hole through both sides of the sashiko in all four places. You can use a specialist screw punch, bradawl or snip in a very small hole with embroidery scissors.

Insert the eyelets into these holes, following the manufacturer's instructions. Line them up carefully. Once you have all of the pieces ready you can start the binding.

Sandwich the inner papers between the card and the sashiko cover, aligning the holes. Place a bulldog clip on each short edge to hold the papers and cover together. Thread the cord onto the tapestry needle. With the sashiko cover facing up, carefully part the top half of the pages at the spine and pass the needle between these pages to the inside of the book and up through hole 2, leaving a 4in (10cm) tail of cord. Take the cord around the spine on the outside of the book and up again through hole 2, from the back cover through the inner pages and out through the front cover ③.

Pass the cord through hole 3, from the front to the back of the book, then around the spine and back through the same hole ④.

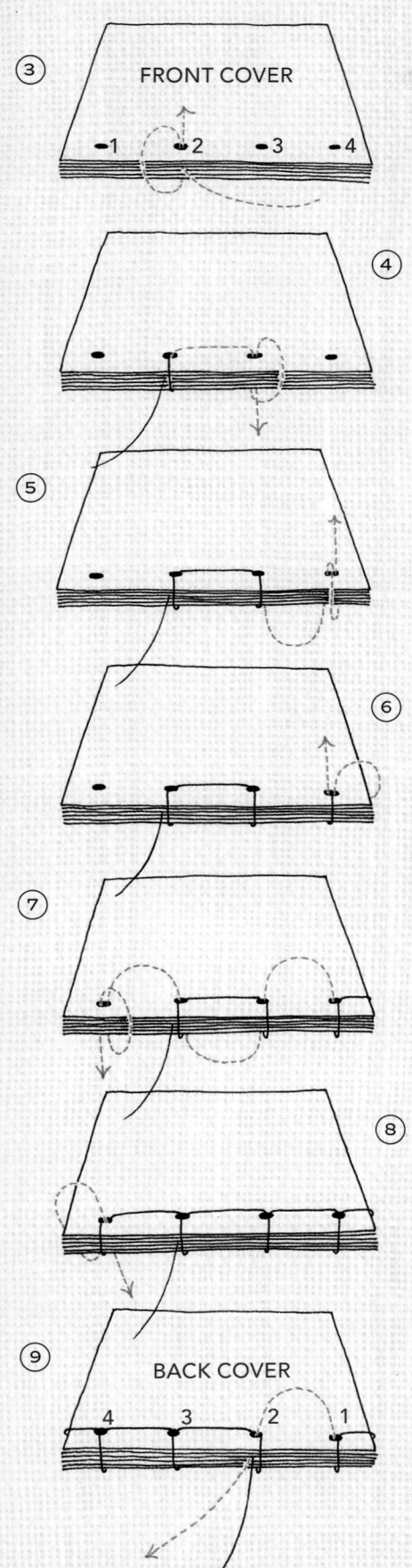

Pass the cord through hole 4 from the back cover to the front, around the spine and back up through the same hole ⑤.

From hole 4, pass the cord parallel to the spine, around the lower edge of the book and back up through hole 4 ⑥.

Pass the cord over the front cover, down through hole 3, up through hole 2, down through hole 1, then around the spine and back down through the same hole ⑦.

From hole 1, pass the cord parallel to the spine, around the top edge of the book and back down through hole 1 ⑧.

Turn the book over so the back cover is facing up and remove the bulldog clips. Pass the cord through hole 2 to the middle of the book where the tail of thread was left at the beginning ⑨. Tie these two threads tightly together and snip off the excess.

Sashiko design shown:
NOSHI (see page 110).

Duvet set

YOU WILL NEED

- Tracing paper or greaseproof paper and pen
- Pattern transferring equipment (see page 11)
- Scissors
- Sewing machine/needle and thread
- Board, such as a quilting mat or cardboard, to help draw a neat design if using the Chaco paper technique
- Duvet cover
- Pillowcases
- Sashiko needle and thread
- Iron
- Iron-on interfacing

TIP
······

Heavy thread counts will make the stitching harder work.

For the sashiko pattern shown here, use the template provided on page 110. Alternatively, you can select a different pattern from the Pattern Library (see pages 104–131) or design your own (see pages 14–15). If necessary, enlarge the design you have chosen on a photocopier. Trace it onto tracing paper or greaseproof paper (see page 17). This makes it easier to reverse the design for better placement on the pillowcases.

For the pillowcases, you will need to cut open the end edge to form a tube; it is therefore easier to use a standard pillowcase rather than the Oxford style that has a border. You do not need to shorten the pillowcase to open it; either remove the stitches or cut through. Having two ends open makes sewing easier to handle and you can stitch your design from the front or reverse. It only means losing ¼in (6mm) of fabric after you have re-stitched the end. If you have the Oxford style of pillowcase, it is easier to transfer your design using the Chaco method (see page 16).

For the duvet cover, getting the position of the design correct is key. Place the cover on the bed and experiment with the positioning. Cutting open the top of the duvet makes it easier to stitch. Because the cover is large it is hard to hold all of the fabric while you stitch. Opening both ends means holding half the amount of fabric. You can choose to stitch the duvet using any of the transfer methods (see pages 16–17). But if you are using the Chaco method, place a board under the chosen position and trace through while it's on the bed. This is a particularly effective method if you have a large design.

Complete the stitching on the pillowcases and duvet cover (see page 20), then iron a piece of fusible interfacing to the reverse of the stitching. This will protect it from regular washing. With right sides together, machine stitch the unpicked ends of the duvet cover and pillowcases, using a ¼in (6mm) seam allowance.

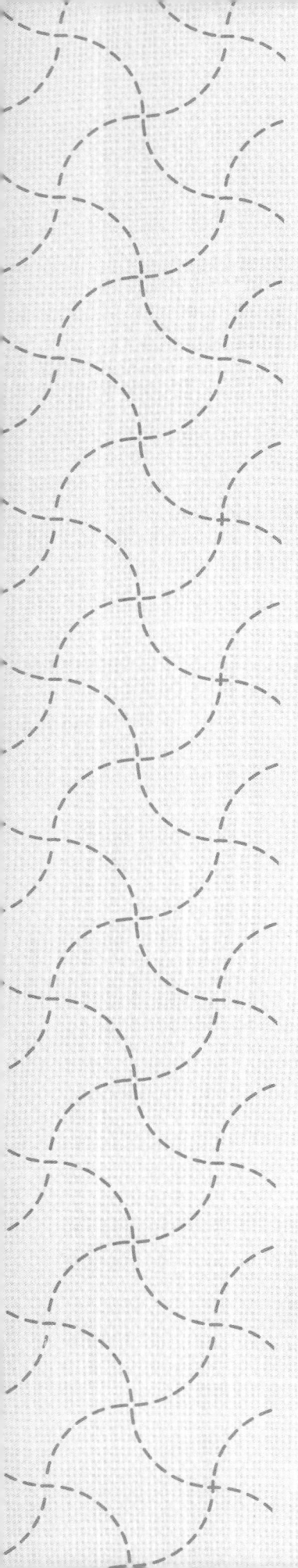

Furoshiki

YOU WILL NEED

- Pattern transferring equipment (see page 11)

- Tailor's chalk

- Freezer paper: 4 pieces, 6 x 6in (15 x 15cm)

- Sashiko fabric, with an even weave to allow fringing: 4 pieces, 10 x 10in (25.4 x 25.4cm)

- Sashiko needle and thread

- Sewing machine and thread (optional)

- Iron

- Featherweight iron-on interfacing: 10in (25.4cm) length

Furoshiki is a type of wrapping cloth used for carrying items such as a lunchbox, when the cloth could also be used as a placemat. This also makes a very pretty reusable gift wrap.

TIP
......

To get the positioning of your stitching perfect, wrap the gift and then mark on the position with tailor's chalk. Unwrap carefully and then stitch.

■ Sashiko fabric – right side

□ Sashiko fabric – wrong side

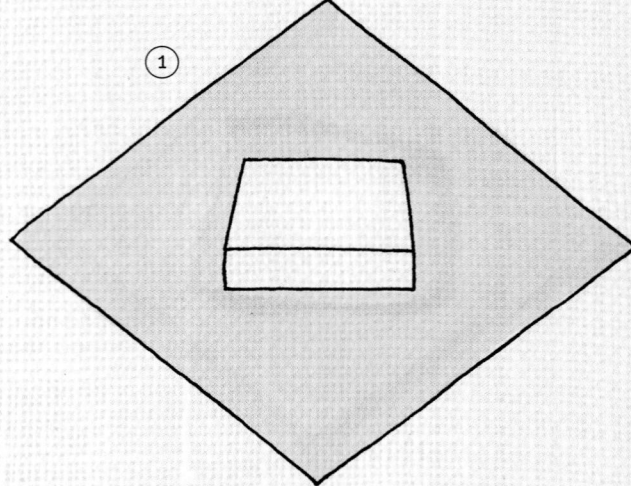

Simple designs are best for furoshiki. Furoshiki are used throughout Japan for everything from carrying shopping to wrapping gifts. For the sashiko patterns shown here, use the templates provided on page 111. Alternatively, you can select a different pattern from the Pattern Library (see pages 104–131) or design your own (see pages 14–15). Transfer the pattern onto the dull side of some freezer paper. Place the design on to the fabric, allowing at least a 1in (2.5cm) seam allowance around the edge if you want to create a fringe around the furoshiki. Place the shiny side of the freezer paper on top of the sashiko fabric and press gently with an iron to temporarily secure it.

Complete the stitching (see page 20), then gently pull off the freezer paper, being careful not to pull the threads. For best results, remove it with two hands, pulling in opposite directions, as if tearing a perforated piece of paper.

If you want to add fringing, stitch a 1in (2.5cm) deep border around the edge, either with sashiko thread or using a sewing machine. Use a needle to carefully pull out a thread parallel to the stitched border on each side of the fabric. Continue until you reach the stitching.

Once fringed, cut a piece of iron-on interfacing to cover the corner you have stitched and hide the back of your sewing. If you have decided not to add a fringe, sew a ¼in (6mm) hem around the edge of your fabric.

With the cloth right side down and the design towards you, place your gift in the centre of your cloth ①.

Bring the back point over and tuck it under the gift ②. Take the front point up and over. You may have to practise to get the design in the position you like.

Pull up both sides neatly ③ and tie once, so the points of the knot are pointing towards the top and bottom of the cloth.

Tie once more. This time, slightly twist the knot so that the points are pointing side to side ④. Don't tie the knot too tight.

To add a bow, simply tuck the points into the knot firmly and arrange into a bow ⑤.

Two seasons scarf

YOU WILL NEED

- Fabric pen
- Featherweight interfacing
- Scissors
- A shawl-style scarf: wide enough to fold in half and not too sheer
- Iron
- Pins
- Ironing cloth to prevent interfacing glue damaging your iron
- Sashiko needle and thread: green and gold for the bamboo, variegated brown/cream for the maple and traditional cream for the 'kantha' style stitching
- Sewing machine/needle and thread

This fabulous scarf is perfect for spring and autumn. The maple leaves are stitched with a lovely brown and cream variegated thread and the bamboo in a fresh lime green and gold for spring.

- ■ Scarf – right side
- ▣ Scarf – wrong side
- □ Interfacing

FOLD LINE

①

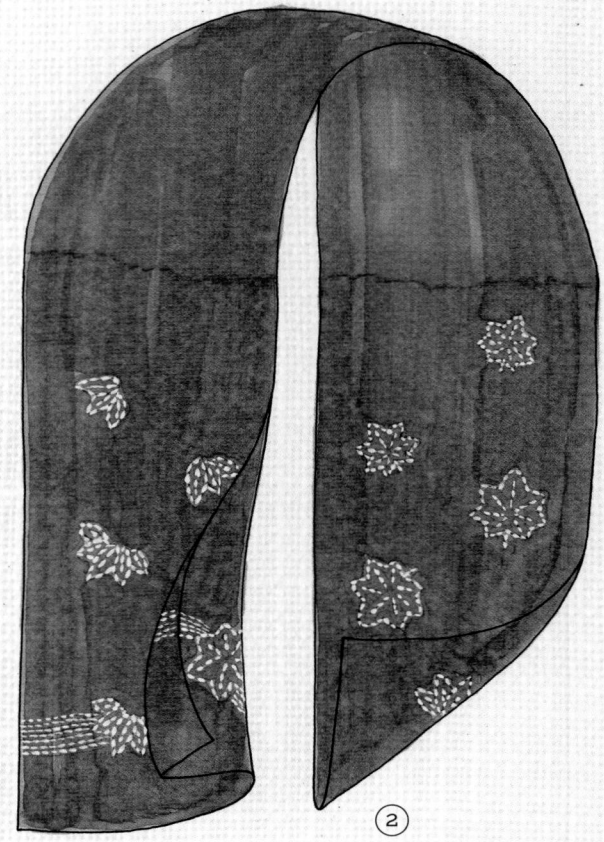

②

Trace three bamboo shapes and two smaller shapes by tracing just three of the leaves (see page 111 for the templates) onto the right (non-adhesive) side of the featherweight interfacing. Now trace three large maple shapes and two smaller ones (see page 111 for the templates). Cut around the shapes neatly, leaving approx. ¼in (6mm) all around.

Iron the scarf in half lengthways. Open this up so that the right side faces down on a flat surface. Take the traced designs and place two matching ones together (adhesive sides on the outside) – one bamboo and one maple. Position the pairs of designs onto one half of your scarf and arrange as desired. Remember these are only on one side of the scarf and will effectively be sandwiched on the inside. Experiment with different placements, and repeat with more designs if required ①.

Pin the designs to one side of the scarf, making sure to place the pins on the outside of the scarf so that they can easily be removed before stitching. Carefully fold the scarf in half. Your designs are now sandwiched between the two sides of the scarf and the pins are on the outside. Place an ironing cloth over the scarf and press until the adhesive has melted a little. Remove the pins and continue pressing until completely stuck down. The designs will now be adhered to the back of the scarf and be perfect mirror images. Open up the scarf and stitch each of the designs (see page 20).

With right sides together, fold the scarf in half lengthways. Line up the shapes and pin them together. Stitch down the long side of the scarf by hand or machine. Remove the pins, turn inside out and again line up the designs, putting in pins to keep them aligned. Give it a final press.

You can add some extra stitching through both layers at this point. It adds a nice, weighted feel to your finished scarf. However, you cannot add a traditional sashiko stitch at this stage: the stitch length would no longer be correct because both sides of the work will be visible. Instead, use a neat and evenly spaced running stitch, so it looks the same on both sides of the scarf. If adding these extra stitches you should plan to finish your stitching at the open bottom end. This is much neater because you can simply hide the finishing stitches or knot them up inside the scarf.

Work carefully and check every few stitches to make sure you are not stitching over the design on the reverse side. Where patterns are slightly different, you can add stitches and fill in gaps by stitching onto the top layer only ②.

Noren door curtain

YOU WILL NEED

- Sashiko fabric: 63 x 36in (160 x 91.5cm)

- Pattern transferring equipment (see page 11)

- Lining fabric: 63 x 36in (160 x 91.5cm)

- Sheet of greaseproof paper or wallpaper lining on a roll: large enough to draw on your chosen design

- Featherweight interfacing: size to fit your chosen design

A noren curtain is a way to separate two rooms without making a physical barrier. They vary greatly in length and width, and are seen in Japanese homes and public spaces.

The design shown here started with a large circle, to which I gradually added lines until I was happy with the result (see pages 112–113 for the templates). I repeated a section of the design in the corners and filled in the panels with two different sashiko patterns (see pages 120 and 131). You can create your own designs (see pages 14–15) or select patterns from the Pattern Library (see pages 104–131).

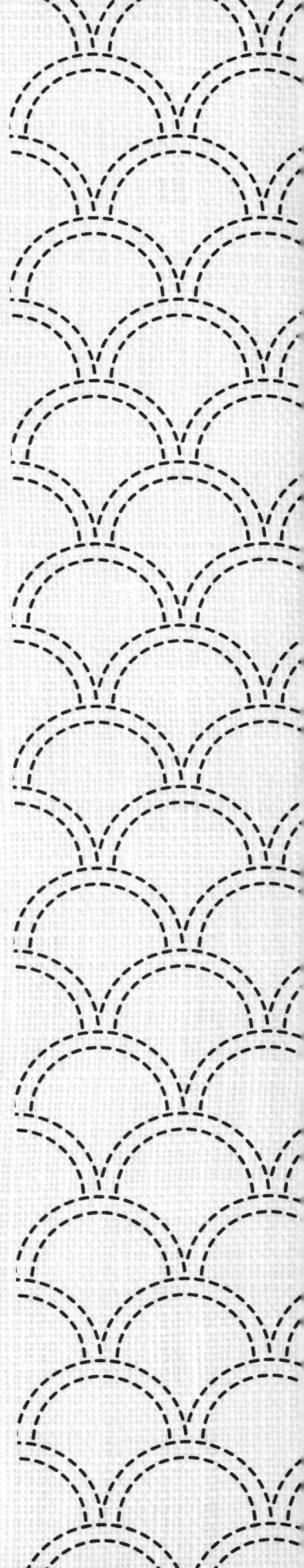

- ▦ Sashiko fabric – right side
- ▢ Sashiko fabric – wrong side
- ▦ Lining fabric – right side
- ▢ Lining fabric – wrong side

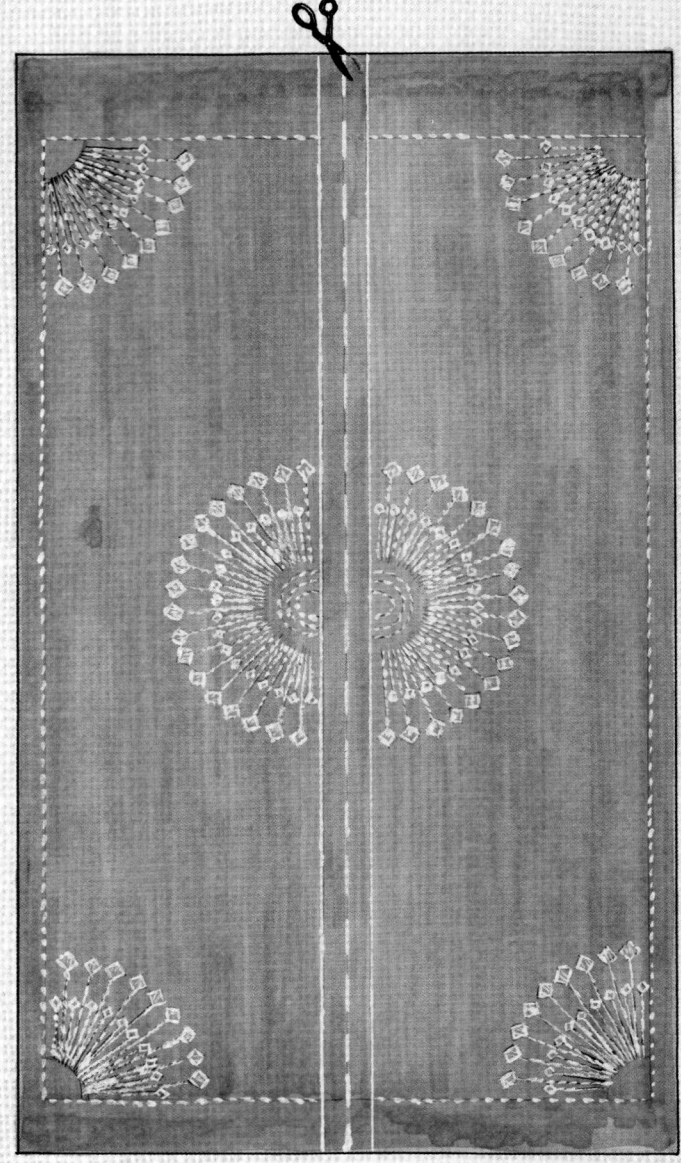

1

On a large sheet of paper, draw out your chosen design for one side of the curtain. Transfer the design onto featherweight interfacing (see page 17). To make a mirror image for the other side of the curtain, place a second piece of interfacing over the first, adhesive sides together, and trace the design.

Fold the sashiko fabric in half lengthways and mark a line down the centre. Open out the fabric and mark a line 1½in (3.8cm) each side of the central line. Transfer the pattern to your sashiko fabric (see pages 16–17). The fabric can be cut in half, following the central marked line, to make it easier to stitch. Complete the stitching (see page 20) 1.

A noren does not always have only two sections. You can add panels together to fit any gap. Put the two stitched panels right sides together and stitch 14in (35.6cm) down the middle 2. Don't press open.

Now cut your lining fabric to exactly the same size. Make the same 14in (35.6cm) row of stitches as your front panel. Cut a small notch as shown in the diagram 3.

With right sides together, pin the sashiko and lining pieces together, matching the seams. Machine stitch together the edges, using a ½in (1.2cm) seam allowance. The notch you cut will make the fabric open wider, to make it easier to sew close to the seam that joined the pieces in the previous step. If you are not confident here, you can slipstitch (see page 21) any small gap left later. Pivot the needle at the seam and continue stitching all the edges together, leaving an 8in (20cm) gap at the top edge for turning through ④.

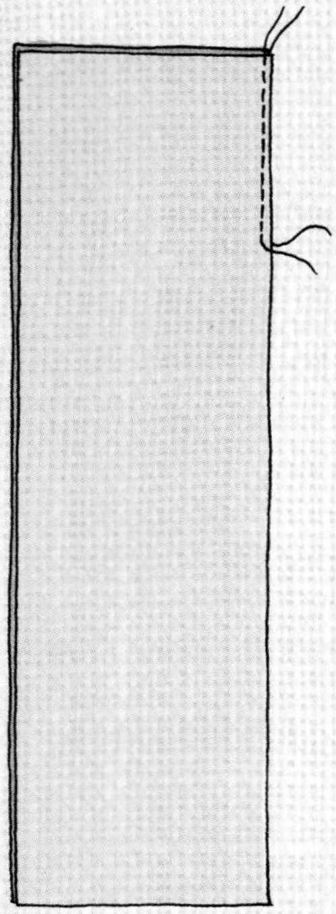

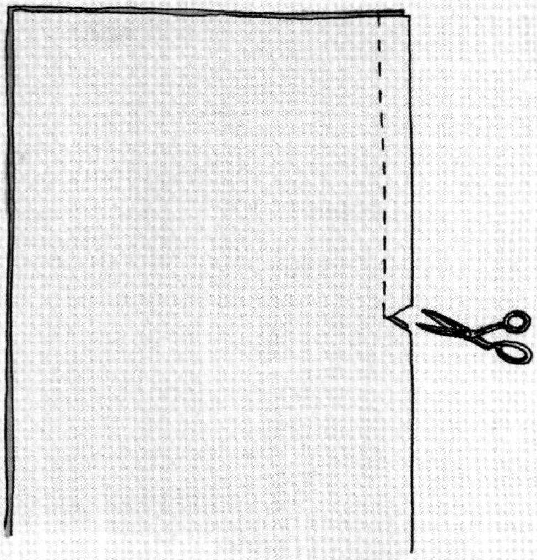

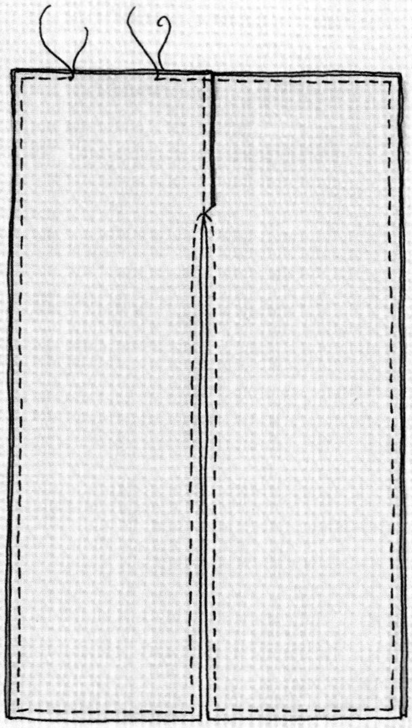

Turn through and press. Slipstitch the opening. Fold down 3in (7.5cm) at the top edge to make a channel for the pole and hand or machine stitch in place ⑤.

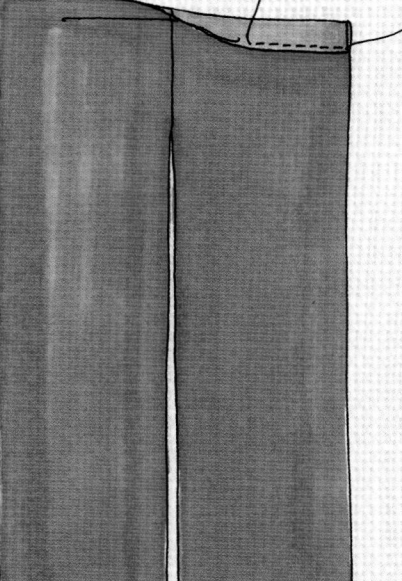

Coin purse

YOU WILL NEED

- Coin purse clasp, half round, sew-in type

- Plain paper for drawing on

- Sharp pencil

- Scissors

- Pins

- Non-permanent pen or tailor's chalk

- Chaco paper

- Quilting mat/cardboard

- Sashiko fabric: size of fabric depends on the clasp chosen

- Lining fabric: lightweight to medium weight, the same size as the outer purse fabric

- Sashiko needle and thread

- Sewing needle and strong thread

- Pins

There are dozens of different variations of the coin purse clasp, which are widely available. They usually do not have a pattern included with them, so you can use the following method to make a pattern for any purse. The same method will also work for glue-in coin purse clasps.

Sashiko design shown:
HOSHI AMI, also known as
FISHING NETS (see page 129).

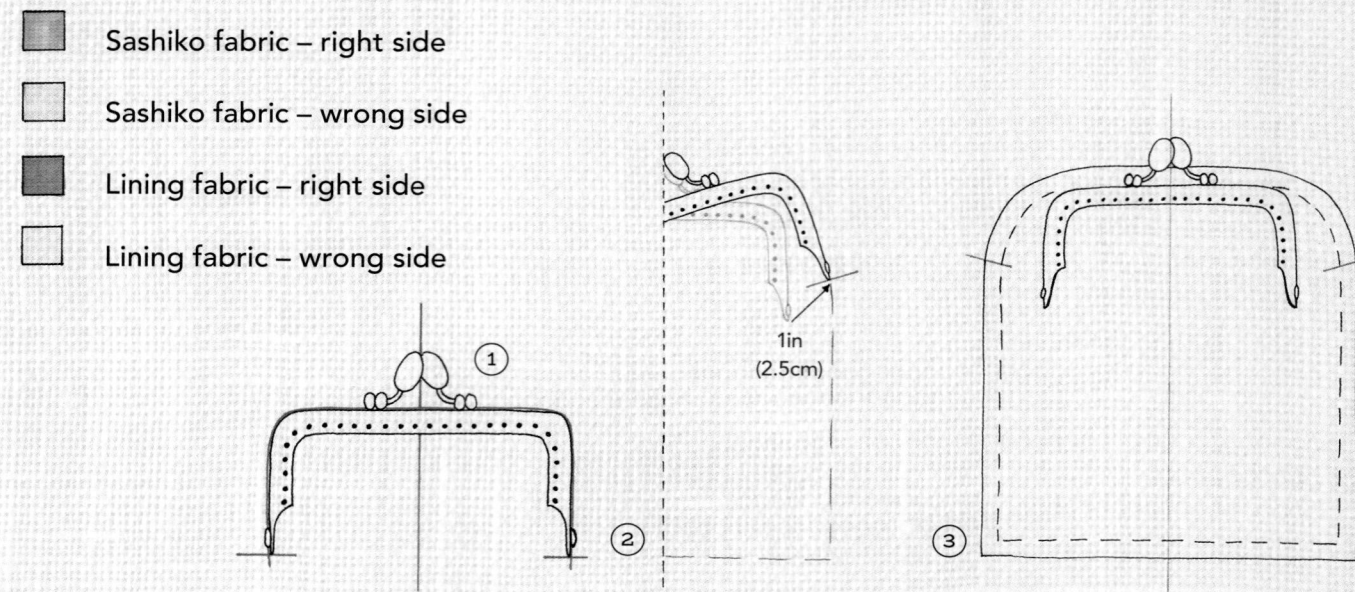

- ▩ Sashiko fabric – right side
- ☐ Sashiko fabric – wrong side
- ▨ Lining fabric – right side
- ☐ Lining fabric – wrong side

Onto a sheet of plain paper, draw around the outer edge of the clasp frame and mark where each end comes with a short line ①. Also mark a line down through the middle.

You need to make the neck of the purse wide enough for fingers. If you make the purse to fit exactly into the clasp it will not be wide enough.

Angle the clasp approximately 1in (2.5cm) out and up and redraw the outer edge. You can now decide which shape and size you would like the purse. I find that curved sides look better with curved frames; however, it's your choice. You only need to do this on one half. You can then fold the paper in half down the centre line and copy onto the other half by tracing. Both halves should be exactly the same ②.

Add a ¼in (6mm) seam allowance all round and cut out your pattern ③.

Once you have the pattern, you need to cut out two pieces of lining fabric and two pieces of sashiko fabric. Mark the red line on all the pieces with a pin or non-permanent pen, or use tailor's chalk.

Pin the two pieces of lining fabric right sides together. Stitch around from one red line to the opposite one around the bottom of the purse, using a ¼in (6mm) seam allowance. Snip the seam to the stitching at the red line on each side ④. This helps by loosening the area when joining the lining and sashiko pieces together later.

Choose your sashiko design from the Pattern Library on pages 104–131 or create your own (see pages 14–15). Using the Chaco paper method (see page 16), transfer the design onto the front of the sashiko fabric. If you want to, you can put the design on both sides of the purse.

Stitch your sashiko pattern onto one or both pieces of the sashiko fabric. Pin the right sides together and repeat as per the lining, stitching as far as the red line.

Turn the liner through, so that the right side is on the outside. Slip the liner inside the sashiko section. You must make sure that the right sides of both the liner and the sashiko are together.

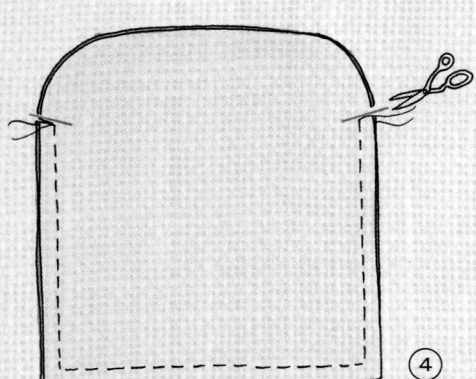 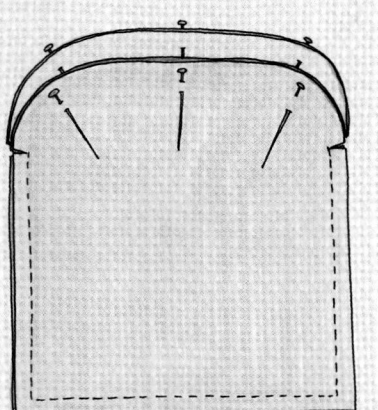 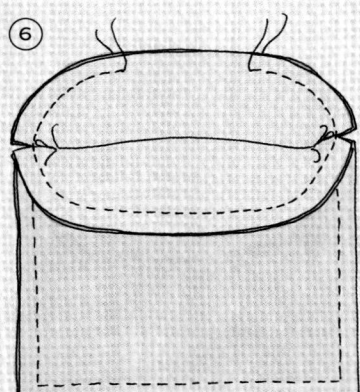

Aligning the raw edges, pin each side of the sashiko and lining together (5).

Sew around the top of the purse, but leave a gap large enough to be able to turn the purse through to the right side (6). This gap will differ slightly for each purse.

To attach the purse frame you will need to find the centre of both sides of the frame and the fabric section. With the frame open, match the centres and, using sewing thread, attach the frame to the purse as shown (7). Do not sew through the holes.

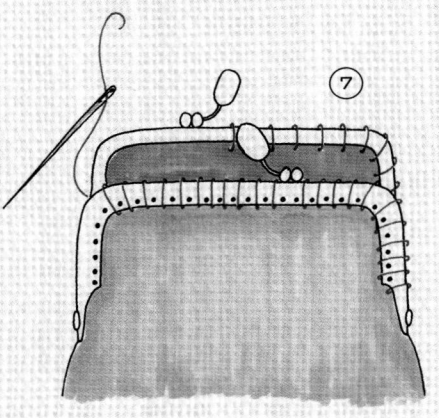

Using your strong thread you can now sew the purse and clasp together. Sew each side separately. Start at the centre of the frame and work each stitch until you get to the hinge, and then turn and work back to the centre, filling in each stitch (8). Continue until all the holes are stitched. Regularly check that it is neat on the inside. Remove the sewing thread used in the previous step.

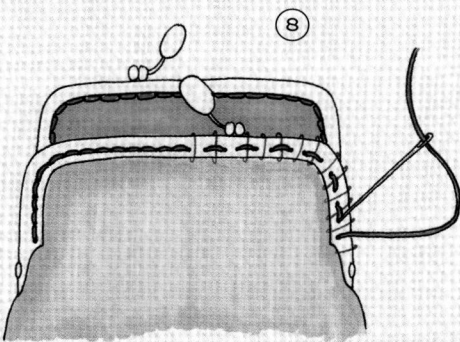

Patchwork bag

YOU WILL NEED

- Pattern transferring equipment (see page 11)
- 3ft (1m) length of ¼in (6mm) wide cord for the drawstring and two beads with a large hole that the cord will thread through
- Sashiko needle and thread
- Sewing machine/needle and thread
- Pins
- Water-erasable or chalk pen
- Iron

FOR THE BAG FRONT:

- Flower pattern fabric: 5 x 14in (12.5 x 35.6cm), cut in 2, to 5 x 7in (12.5 x 17.8cm)
- Brown pattern fabric: 6 x 21in (15 x 53.3cm), cut into 3, to 6 x 7in (15 x 17.8cm)
- Plain brown fabric: 5 x 14in (12.5 x 35.6cm), cut in 2, to 5 x 7in (12.5 x 17.8cm)

FOR THE BAG TOP AND BOTTOM:

- Plain brown fabric: 2 pieces, 3½ x 10in (9 x 25.4cm)

FOR THE BAG BACK:

- Plain brown fabric: 10 x 15in (25.4 x 38cm)

FOR THE LINER:

- Blue patterned fabric: 2 pieces, 10 x 15in (25.4 x 38cm)

Sashiko design shown:
MANEKI NEKO (see page 113).

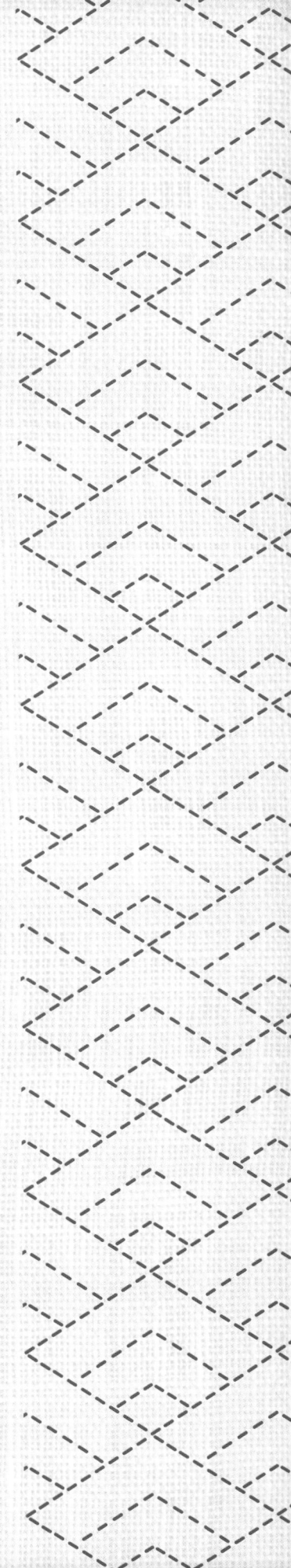

- ■ Brown pattern fabric – right side
- ■ Brown pattern fabric – wrong side
- ■ Flower pattern fabric – right side
- ■ Flower pattern fabric – wrong side
- ■ Plain brown fabric – right side
- ■ Plain brown fabric – wrong side
- ■ Liner fabric – right side
- ■ Liner fabric – wrong side

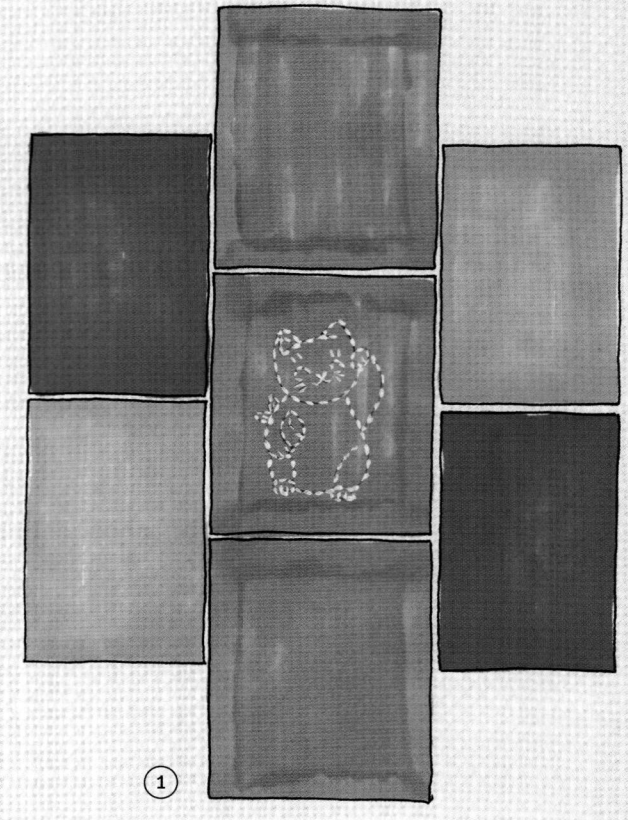

①

Trace the template on page 113. Alternatively, select a pattern from the Pattern Library (see pages 104–131) or design your own (see pages 14–15).

Transfer the design (see pages 16–17) to one of the 6 x 7in (15 x 17.8cm) brown patterned pieces and complete the stitching (see page 20).

Lay out your fabrics as shown ①. With right sides together and using a ¼in (6mm) seam allowance, stitch each of the two side pieces together, and the three centre pieces together, to make three vertical strips of patchwork. Open up the joined pieces and press the seams open. With right sides together, sew the side panels to the centre panel as they were laid out in the first step, using a ¼in (6mm) seam allowance to make one panel. Press the seams open.

Cut out a 10in (25.4cm) square from a piece of paper. Lay it over the patchwork and position it so the whole square fits inside your piece of fabric ②. The 10in (25.4cm) includes your seam allowance.

With right sides together and using a ½in (1.2cm) seam allowance, stitch the top and bottom pieces to the top and lower edges of the patchwork panel, and the back piece to the bottom piece. With right sides together, stitch a lining piece to each end of the strip as shown ③.

Fold the sewn strip in half right sides together and pin. On both sides, mark a 1in (2.5cm) opening in the bag top for the cord channels. Sew a ½in (1.2cm) seam all around, between the cord channels. Leave a 3in (7.5cm) opening in the lining for turning through and backstitch at the beginning and end of each cord channel ④.

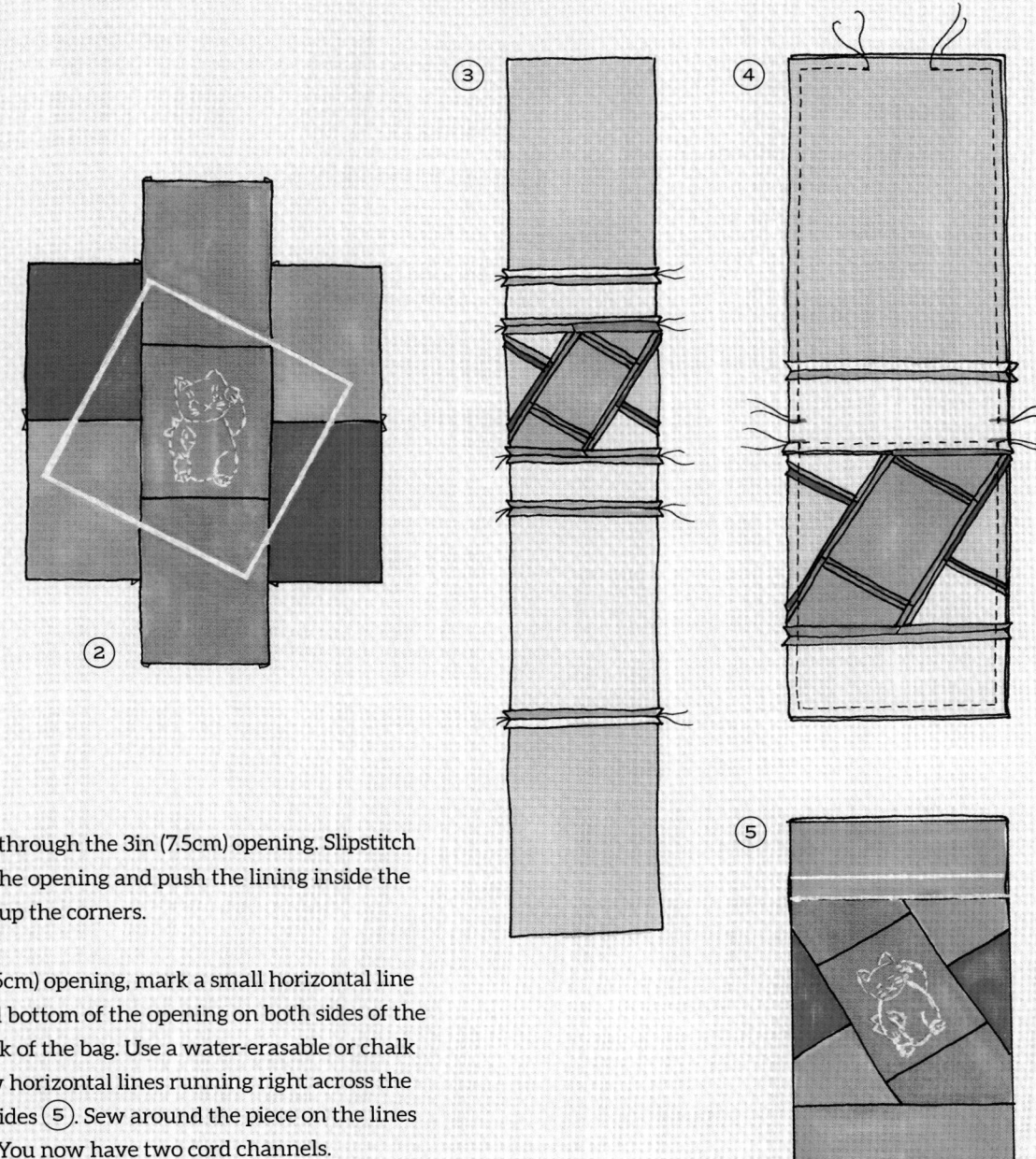

Turn the bag through the 3in (7.5cm) opening. Slipstitch (see page 21) the opening and push the lining inside the bag to match up the corners.

At the 1in (2.5cm) opening, mark a small horizontal line at the top and bottom of the opening on both sides of the front and back of the bag. Use a water-erasable or chalk pen and draw horizontal lines running right across the bag on both sides ⑤. Sew around the piece on the lines you marked. You now have two cord channels.

Cut the cord in half. Thread one half through one channel, all the way around the bag through the channel on the other side and back through the same opening. Thread both ends on the bead and tie the cord in a knot to secure. Repeat with the other half of the cord, threading it through the opening on the other side.

Japanese crossover apron

YOU WILL NEED

- Pattern pieces on pages 98–101 or download a printable PDF (go to: www.gmcbooks.com/books/sashiko)

- Photocopier or tracing paper

- Plain paper

- Scissors

- Clear tape

- Old sheeting (optional)

- Medium-weight main fabric (suitable for washing): for medium size, 79in (200cm) of 36in wide fabric

- Pins

- Sewing machine and thread

- Iron

- Chalk pen

- Sashiko needle and thread

- Featherweight interfacing

TIP
......

It is advisable to mock up the apron using old sheeting so as to know exactly how much fabric you need and ensure the straps are the correct length for you.

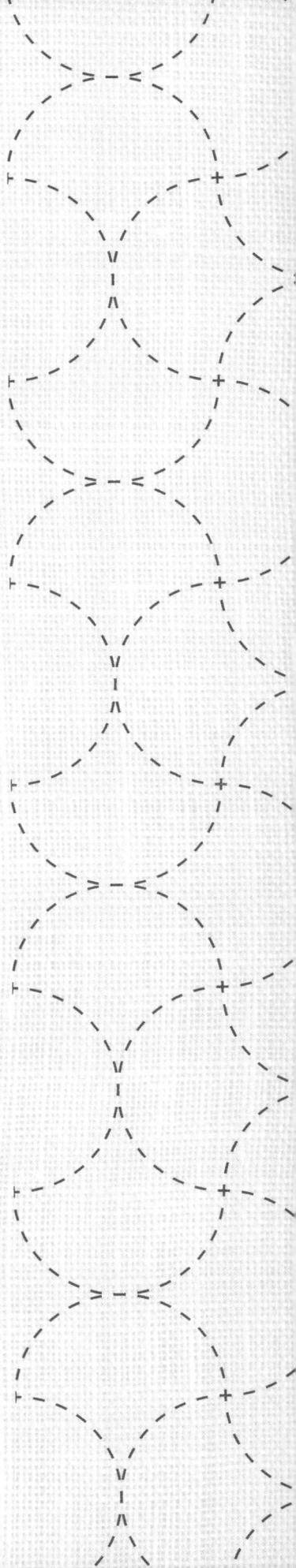

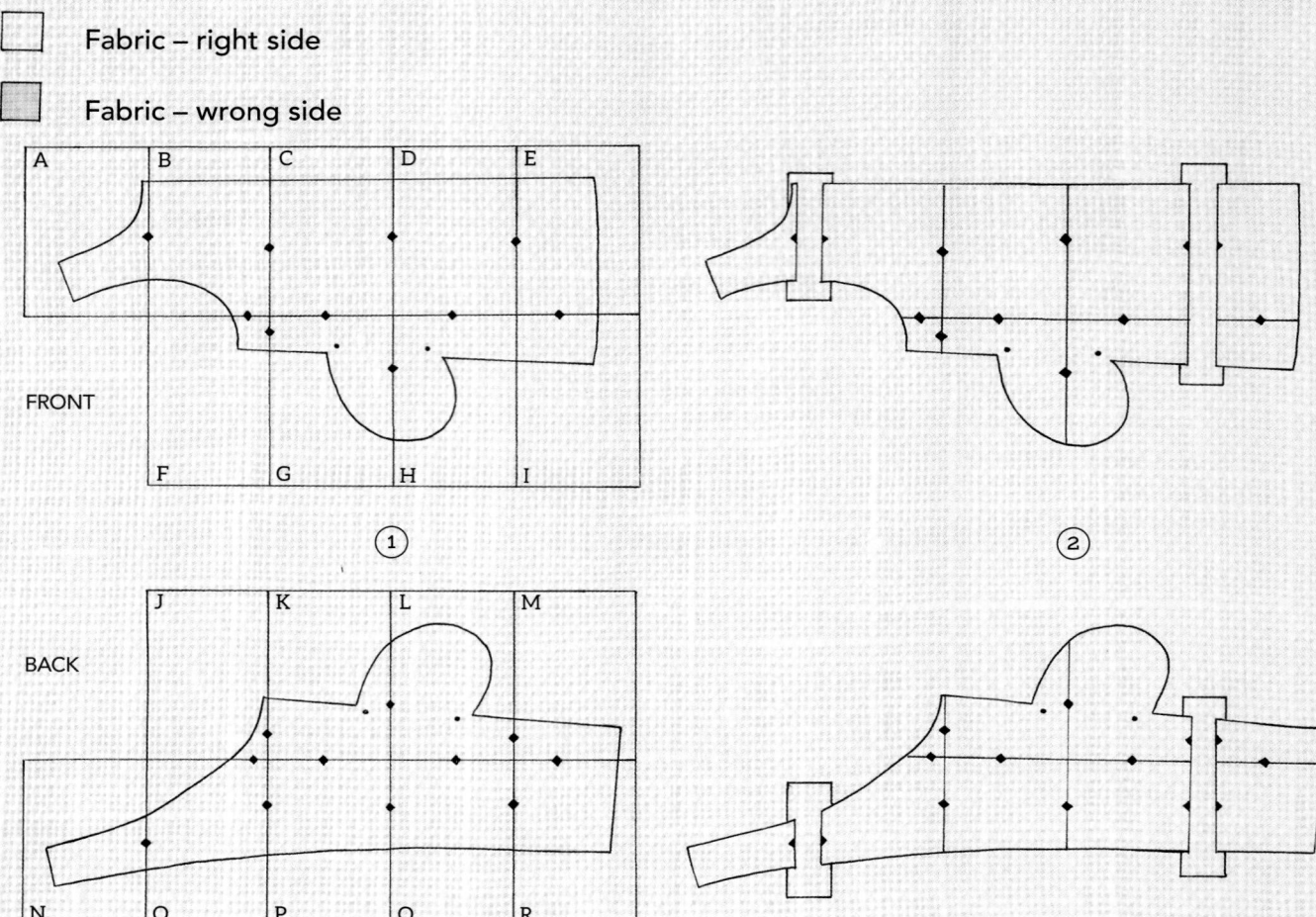

☐ Fabric – right side

▦ Fabric – wrong side

FRONT

BACK

The finished medium-size apron is approximately 21¾in (55cm) wide from underarm to underarm and 35in (89cm) long from shoulder to hem at front. Go to www.gmcbooks.com/books/sashiko for a printable PDF of the pattern pieces. Alternatively, photocopy or trace all the pattern pieces on pages 98–101 at 100%. Cut out each rectangle so that you have 18 pattern pieces. Copy each of the pieces at 300% onto A3-size (29.7 x 42cm/11¾ x 16½in) pieces of paper. The front apron pieces are labelled A–I, with numbered markings 1–10. The back apron pieces are labelled J–R, with numbered markings 11–21. Place the pieces together as shown, matching the numbered markings ①. Join them together using clear tape, with no overlaps at the edges. Cut out the taped pattern.

To lengthen the apron at the top or bottom, insert a strip of paper between the horizontal join of the pattern with more paper ②. Trim the excess paper at the edges.

To shorten the apron, overlap the horizontal strips evenly, at the top or bottom, to the desired length ③. Make sure both the front and back pattern pieces are adjusted to the same measurement.

To make the apron wider, insert a strip of paper between the two vertical strips of the pattern with more paper ④.

To make the apron narrower, overlap the two vertical strips to the desired width. Trim the excess paper, to create a smooth line, if necessary ⑤.

Fold the fabric in half widthways, right sides together, and pin the pattern pieces to the fabric ⑥.

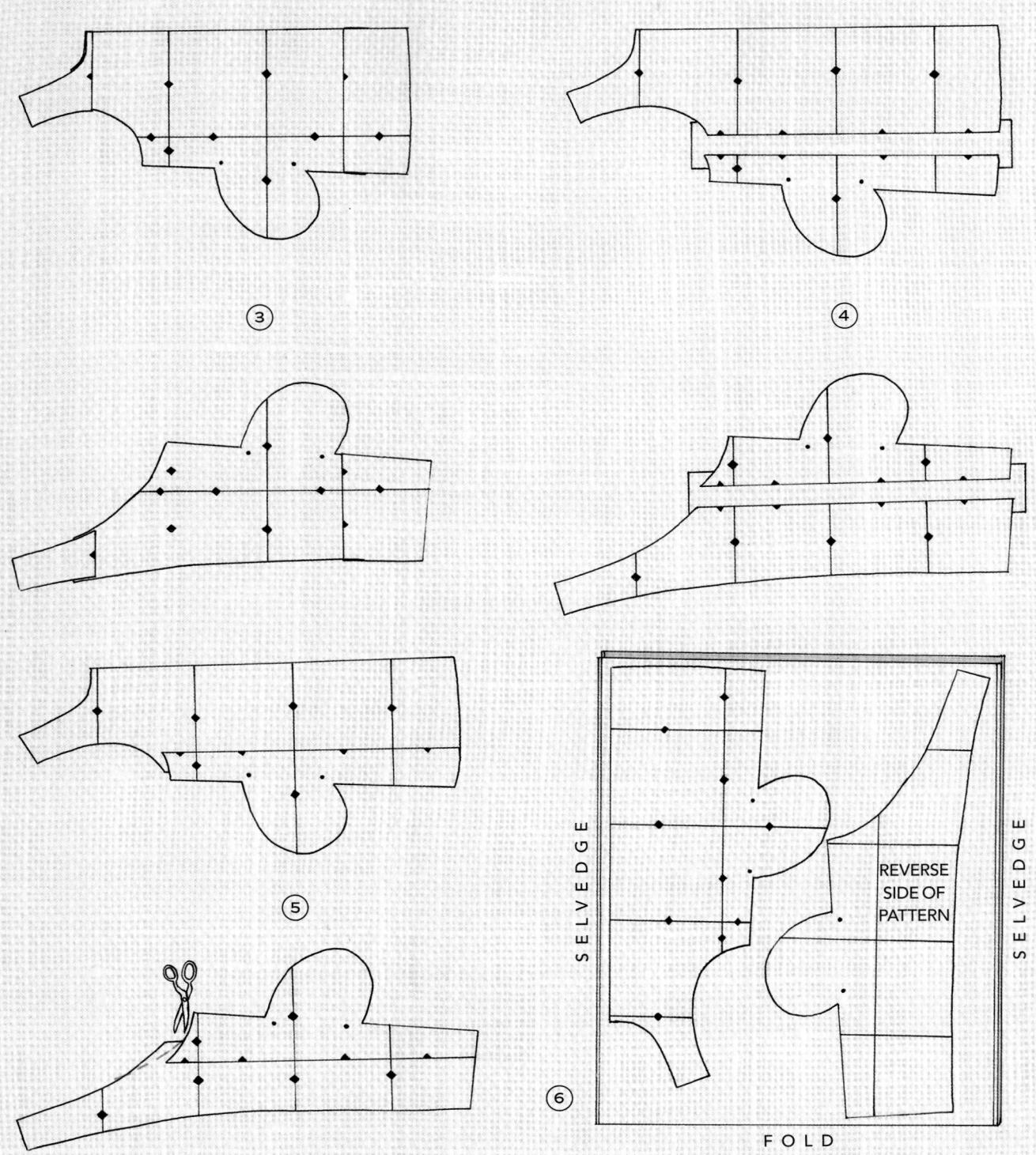

③

④

⑤

⑥ REVERSE SIDE OF PATTERN

SELVEDGE

SELVEDGE

SELVEDGE

FOLD

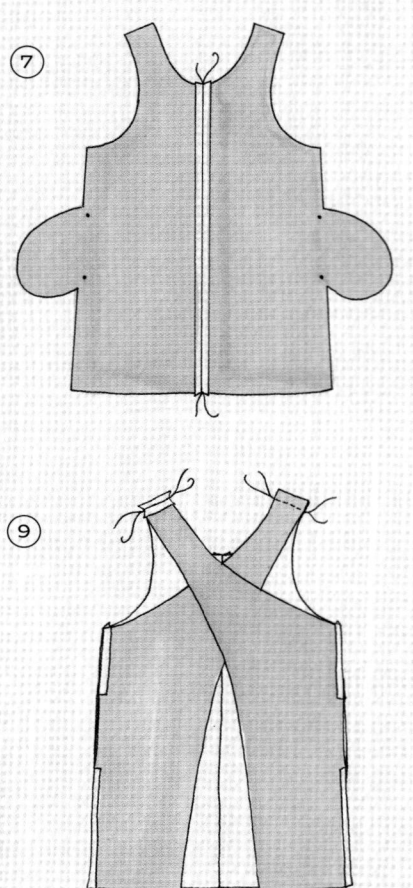
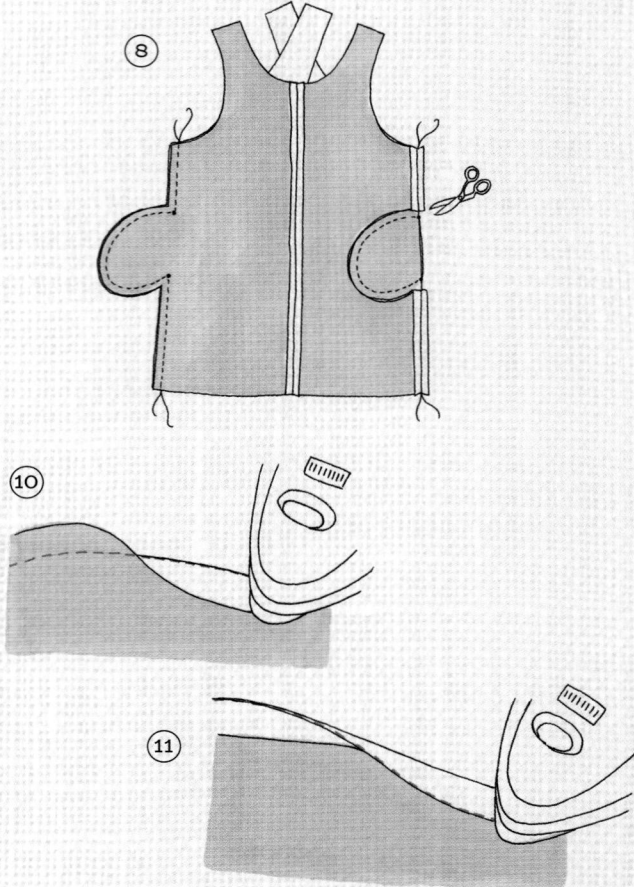

Cut out the fabric and transfer the dots to the fabric pockets, as indicated on the pattern, with a chalk pen. With right sides together, stitch together the centre front, using a ½in (1.2cm) seam allowance. Press open the seam ⑦.

With right sides together, using a ½in (1.2cm) seam allowance, pin and stitch the back pieces to the front, pivoting the needle at the dots around the pocket. Snip the seam allowance on the apron back at the top and bottom of the pocket, taking care not to cut into the stitching. Turn each pocket towards the front of the apron and press ⑧.

With right sides together, pin the straps in place. Put on your apron and adjust the straps as needed. Stitch together using a ½in (1.2cm) seam allowance. Press the seams open ⑨.

Now you have a completed apron, you can add some sashiko. You will be turning under a hem so start your design no less than ½in (1.2cm) in from the edges. You can use the templates

on page 113, select a different pattern from the Pattern Library (see pages 104–131) or design your own (see pages 14–15). Transfer the design to the apron (see pages 16–17) and complete the stitching (see page 20). Once your sashiko is finished you can cut a piece of featherweight interfacing to fit over the patterns or simply leave. Adding the interfacing gives strength to the stitching when washed.

To finish the armholes, neck and hem of the apron, stitch a line of basting ¼in (6mm) from the raw edge, all the way around your hem. The basting measures and marks a precise ¼in (6mm) for you, so you don't have to do a lot measuring and marking by hand. It forms a hard line, making the hem easier to fold over and it makes it easier to fold under twice. On the wrong side, turn along the basting and press ⑩. Once your hem is pressed, turn again and press ⑪. The raw edge should be up against the bottom fold, within the hem and very neat. Pin and sew around the hem. Because of the surface area, a sewing machine is preferable.

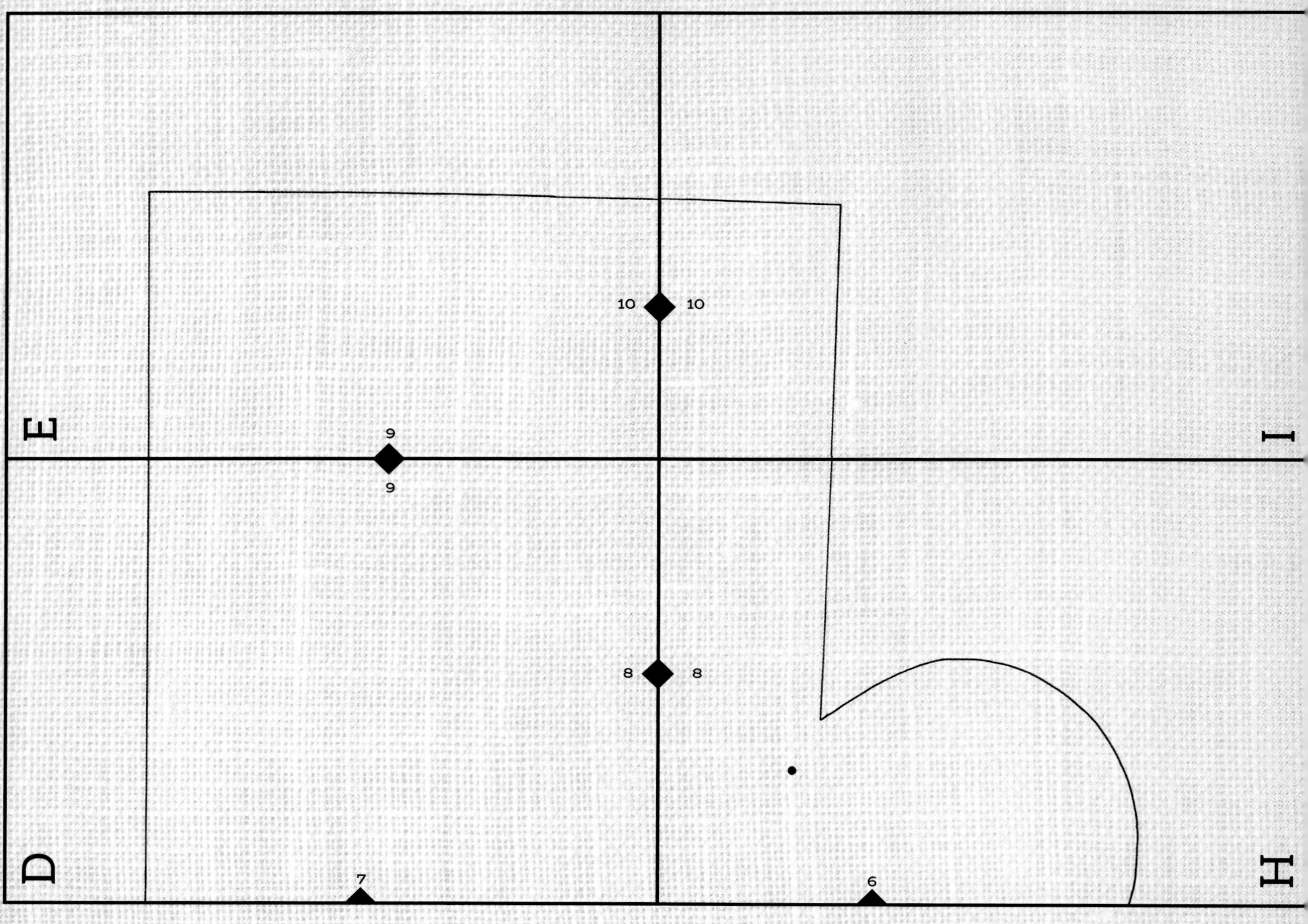

E   I

10 ◆ 10

9 ◆ 9

8 ◆ 8

D   H

7

6

FRONT OF APRON

Photocopy or trace the pattern pieces at 100%. Pattern pieces include ½in (1.2cm) seam allowance. Cut out each rectangle so that you have 9 pattern pieces. Copy each of the pieces at 300% onto A3-size (29.7 x 42cm/11¾ x 16½in) paper. Place the pieces together as shown in the illustration on the right, matching the numbered markings. Join them together using clear tape, with no overlaps at the edges.

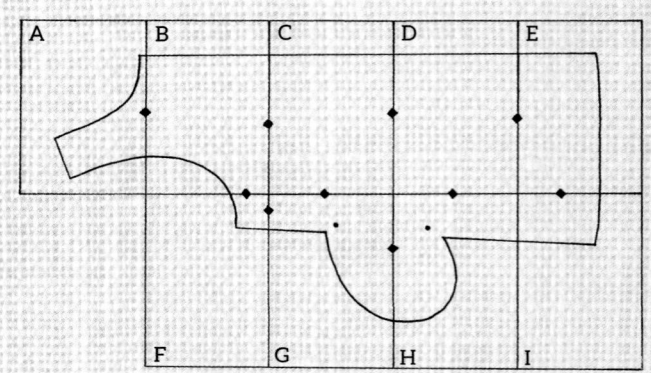

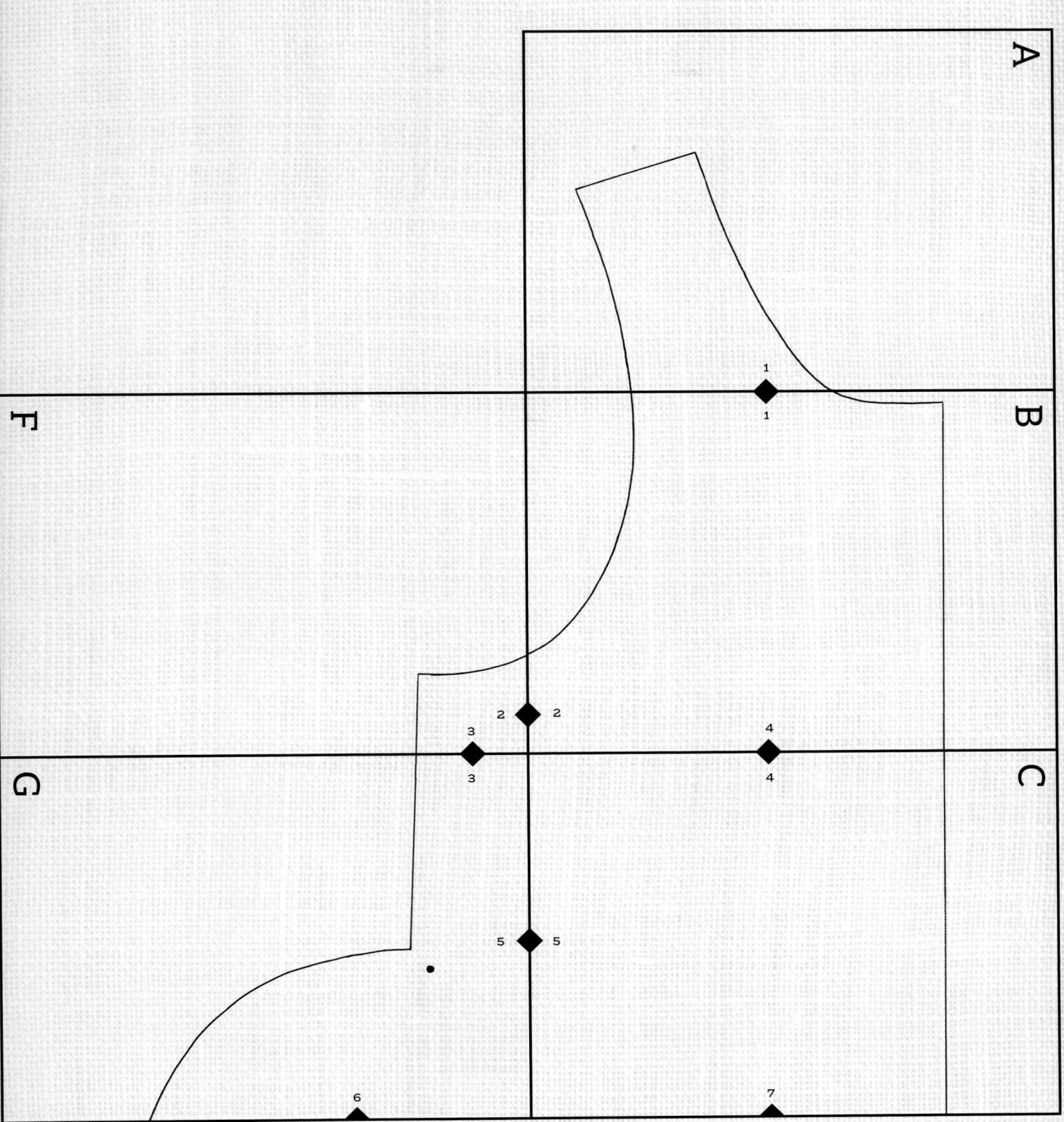

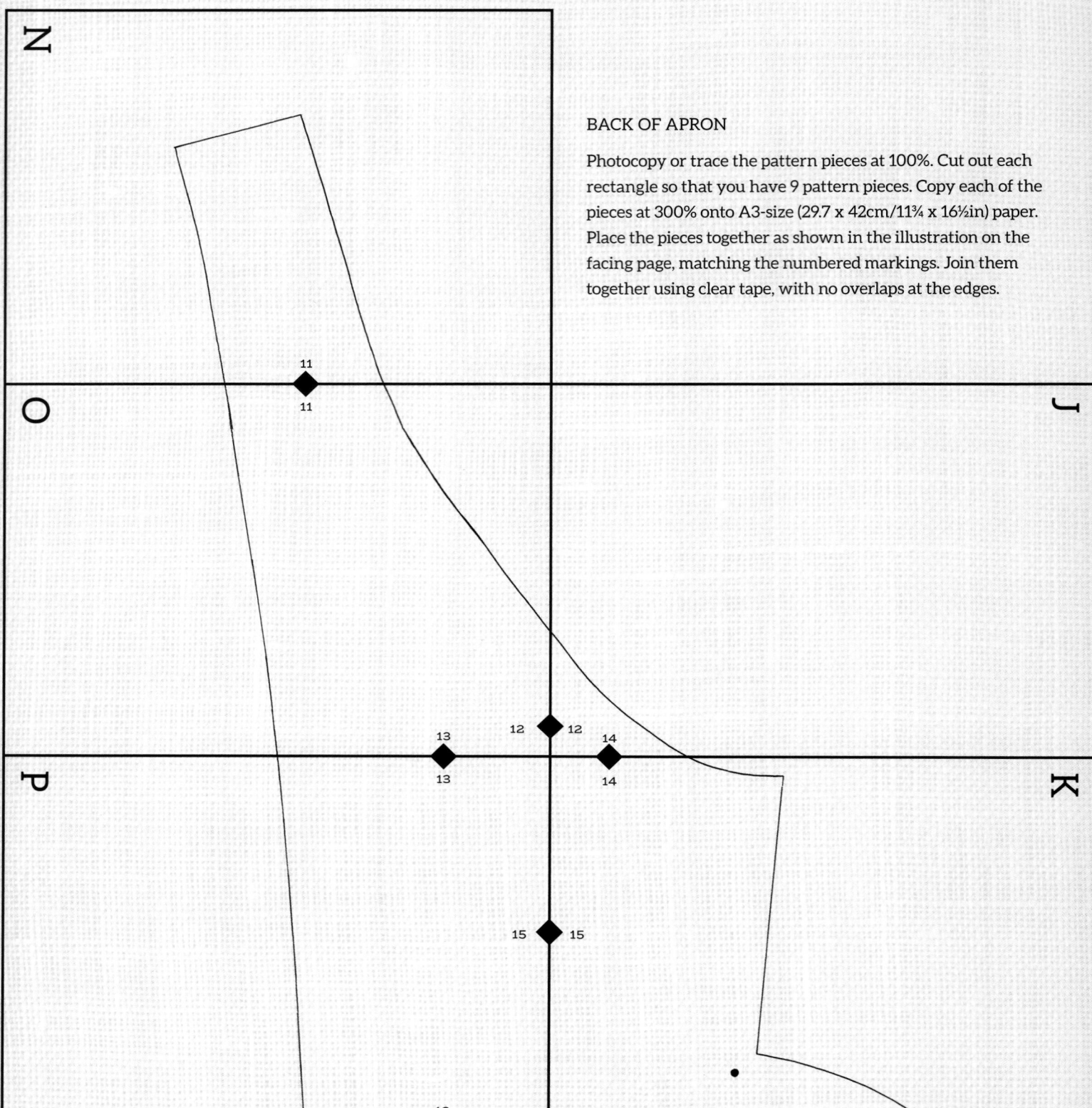

BACK OF APRON

Photocopy or trace the pattern pieces at 100%. Cut out each rectangle so that you have 9 pattern pieces. Copy each of the pieces at 300% onto A3-size (29.7 x 42cm/11¾ x 16½in) paper. Place the pieces together as shown in the illustration on the facing page, matching the numbered markings. Join them together using clear tape, with no overlaps at the edges.

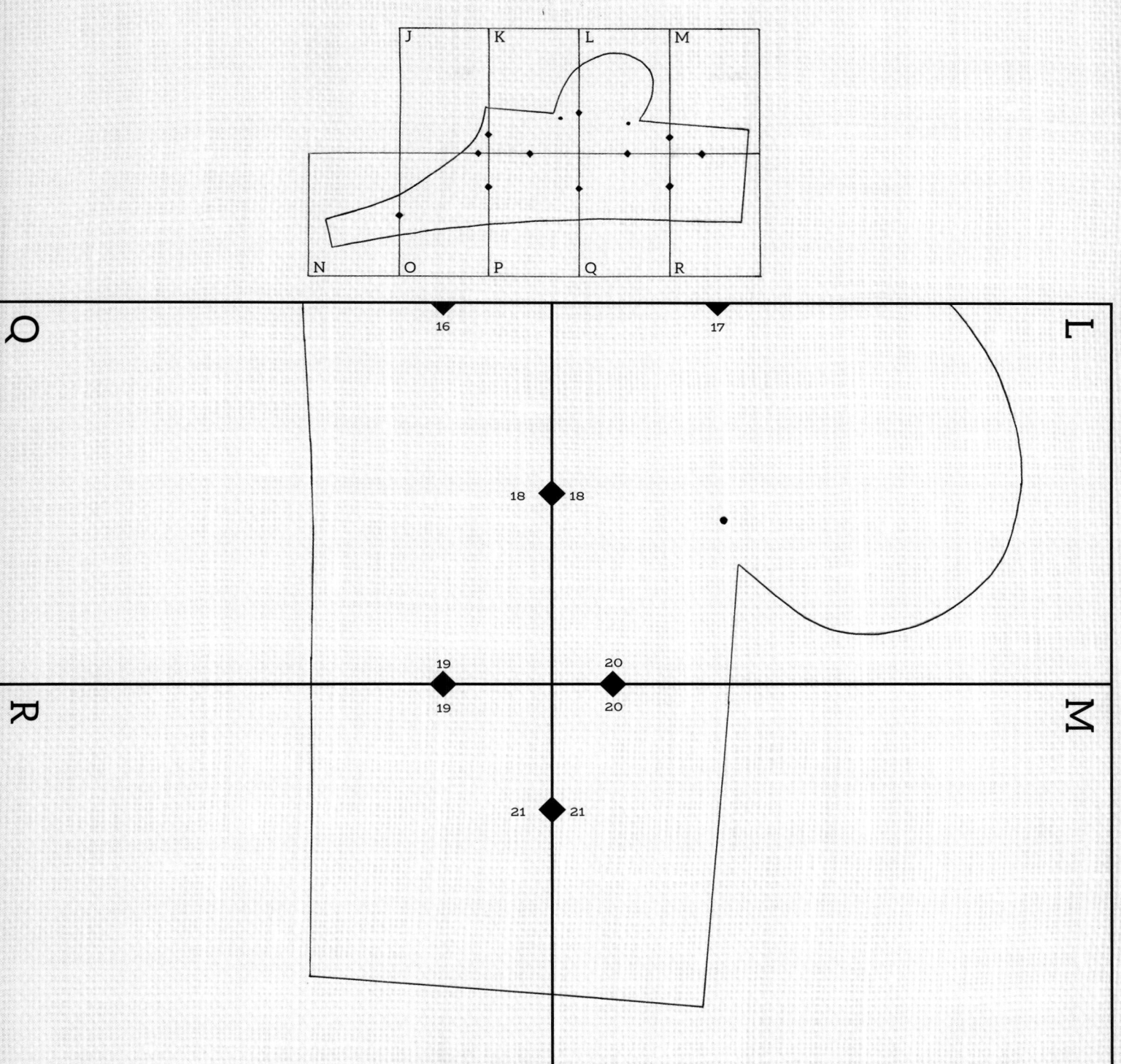

Pattern library

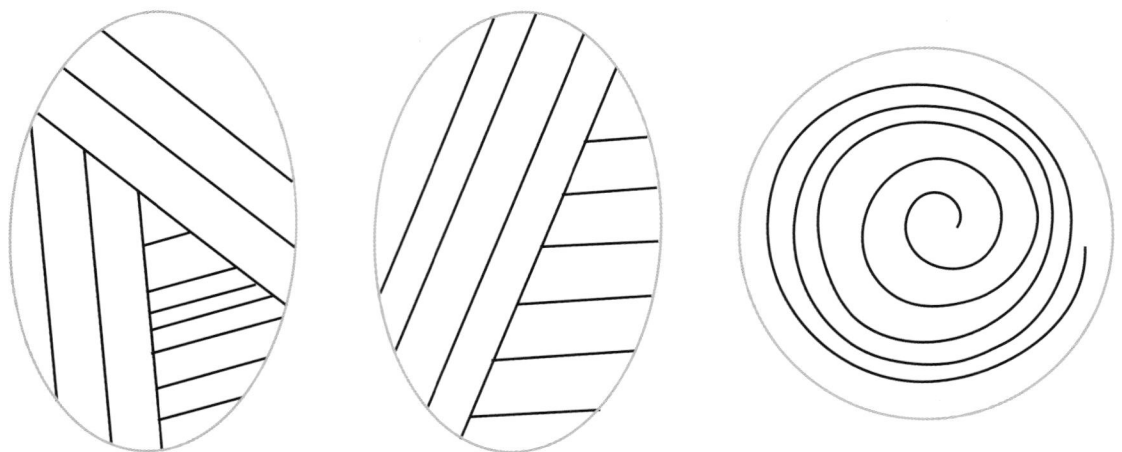

TABLEMATS (page 28) Copy at 150%

BOOK COVER (page 42). Copy at 100%

PLUM BLOSSOM
(see Needle Case, page 38)
Copy at 150%

CUSHION COVER
(page 50)
Copy at 150%

BAMBOO
(see Wall Hanging, page 54)
Copy at 200%

TABLE RUNNER
(page 58)
Copy at 150%

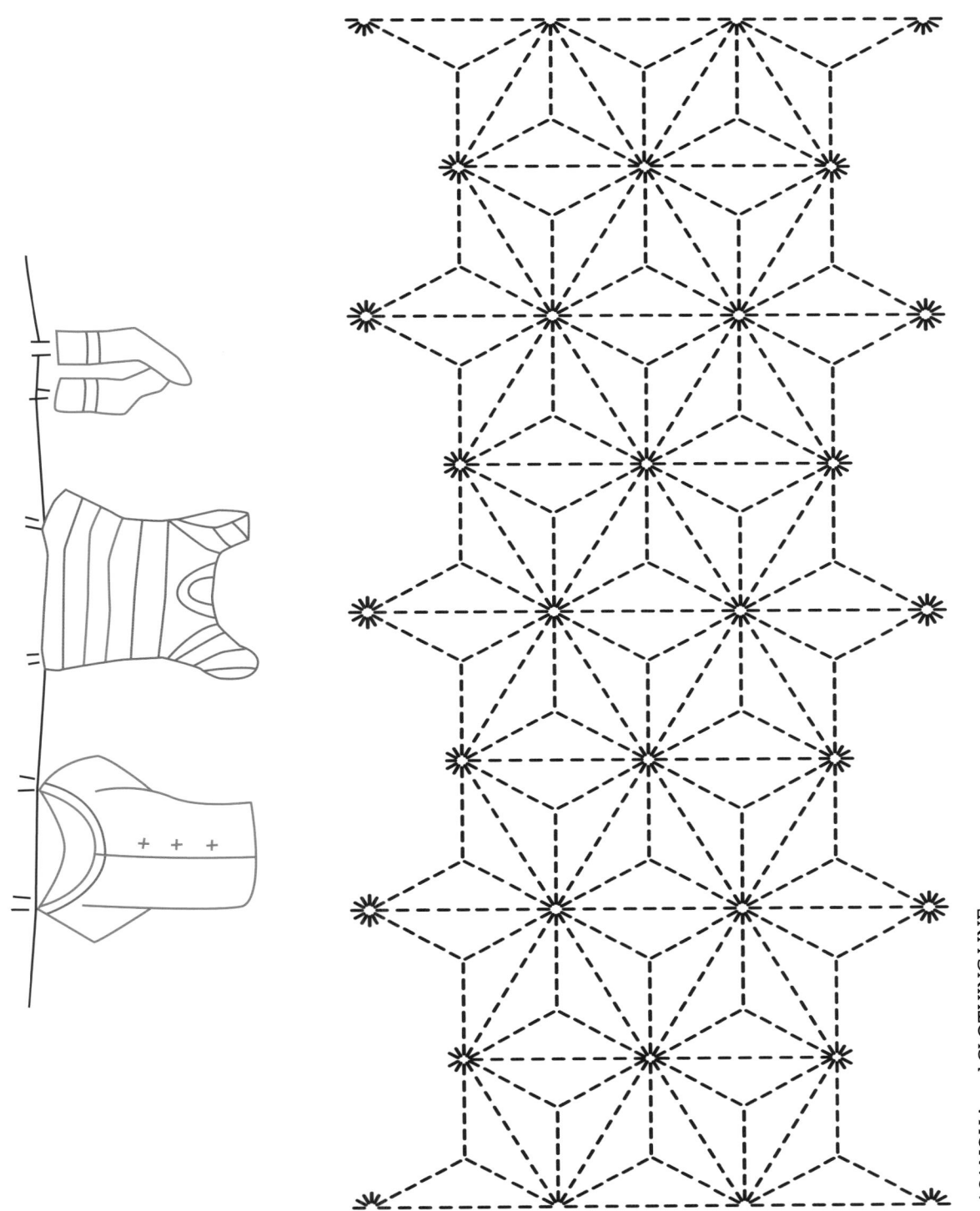

ASANOHA and CLOTHING LINE
(see Laundry Bag, page 62).
Copy at 200%

NOSHI
(see Duvet Set, page 70)
Copy at 150%

FUROSHIKI
(page 72)
Copy at 100%

TWO SEASONS SCARF
(page 76)
Copy at 150%

NOREN DOOR CURTAIN
(page 80)
Copy at 200%

NOREN DOOR CURTAIN
(page 80)
Copy at 200%

MANEKI NEKO
(see Patchwork Bag, page 88)
Copy at 200%

JAPANESE CROSSOVER APRON
(page 92)
Copy at 150%

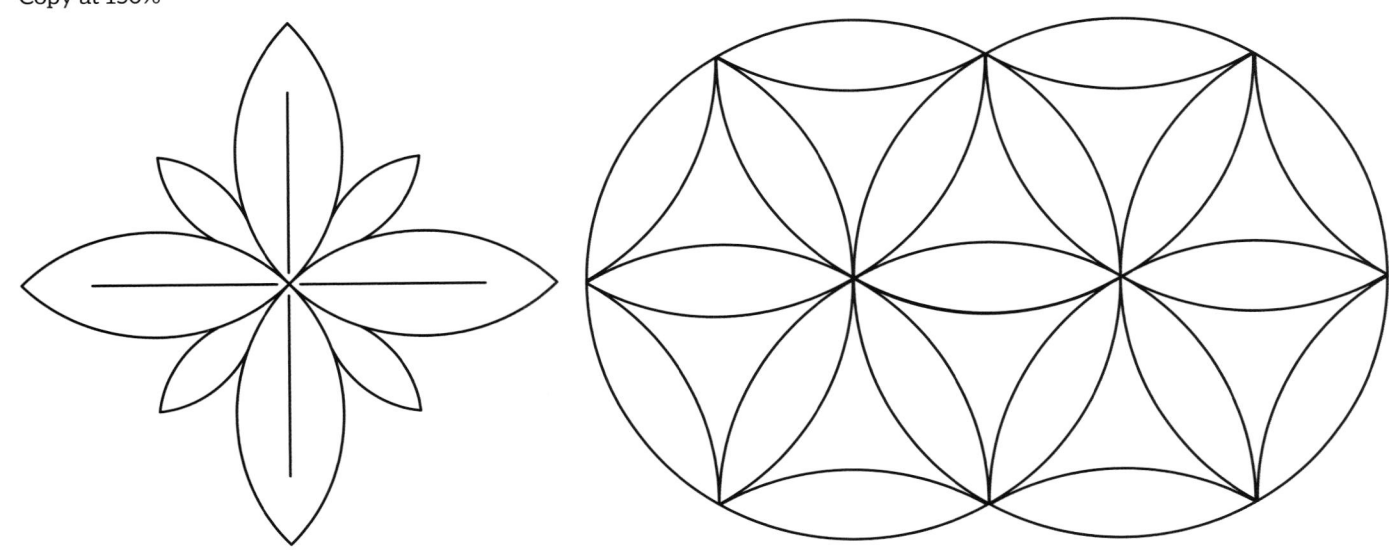

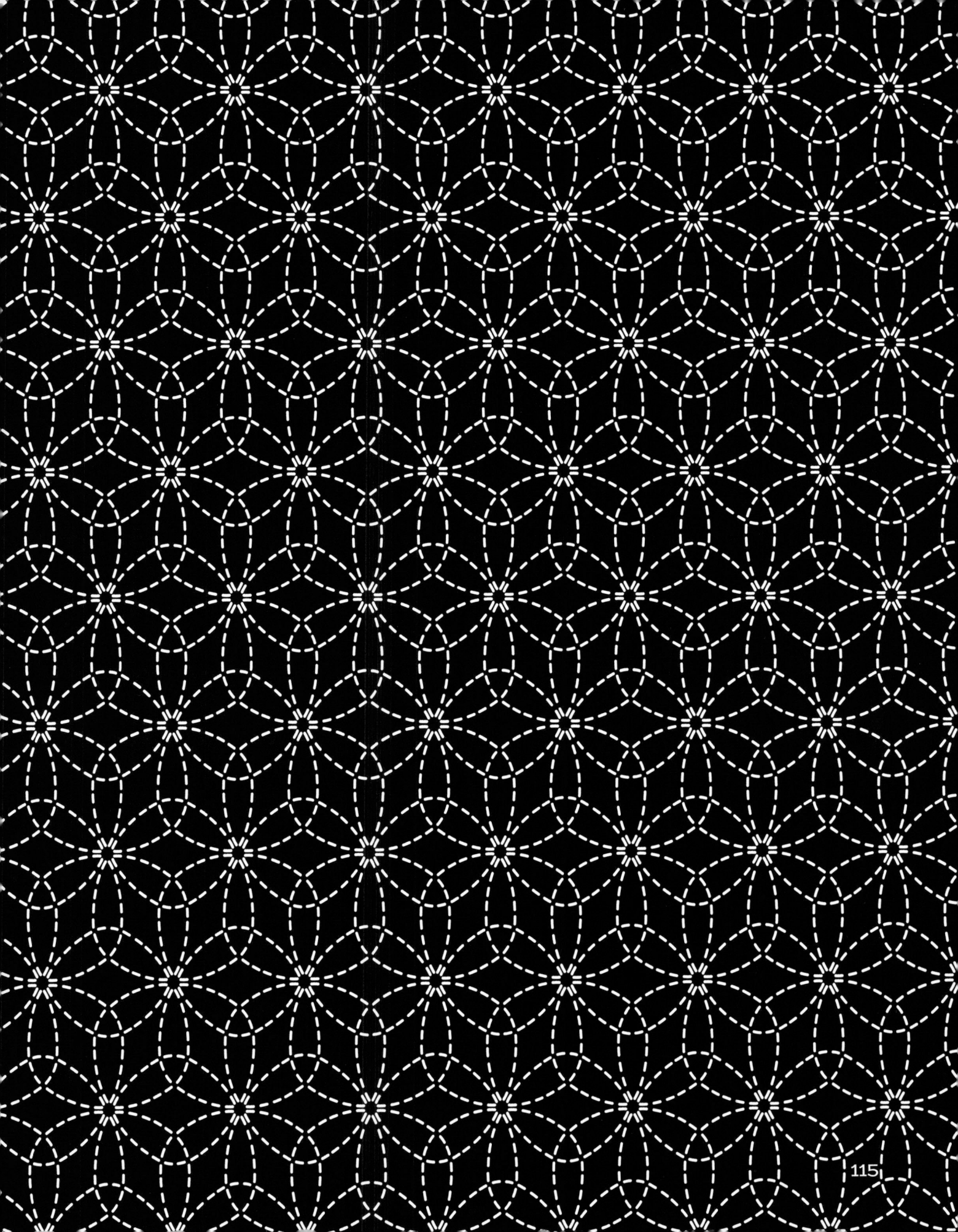

118

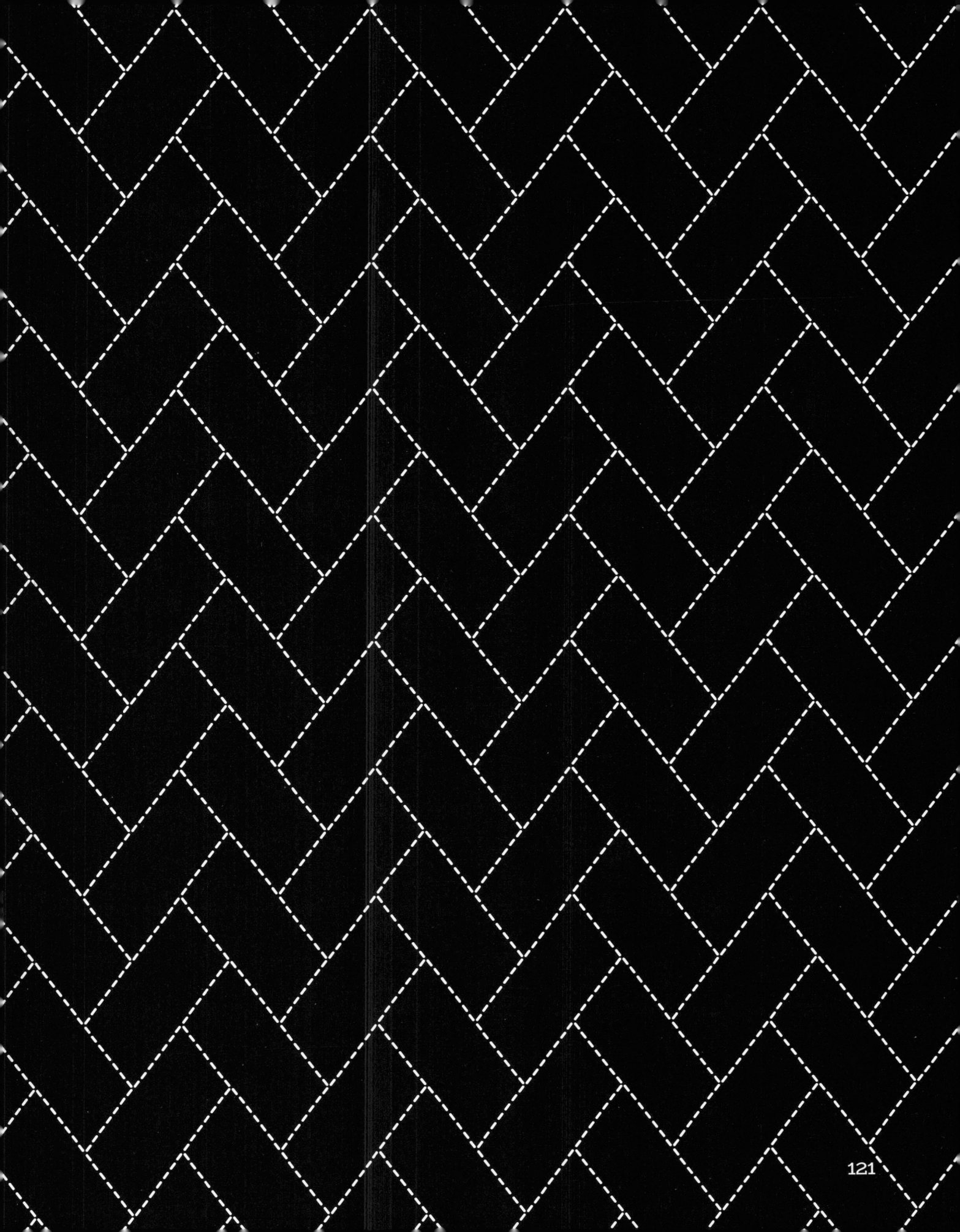

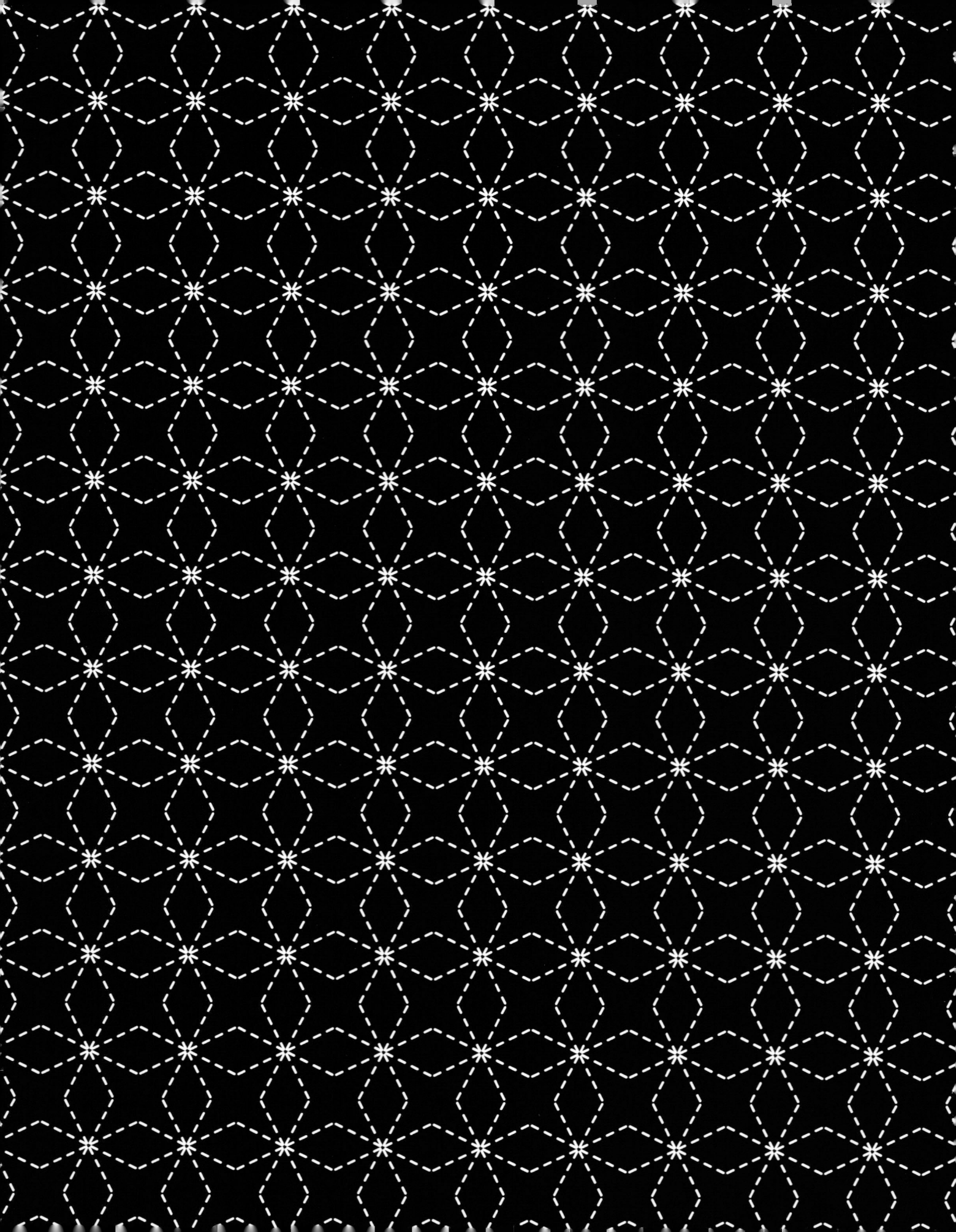

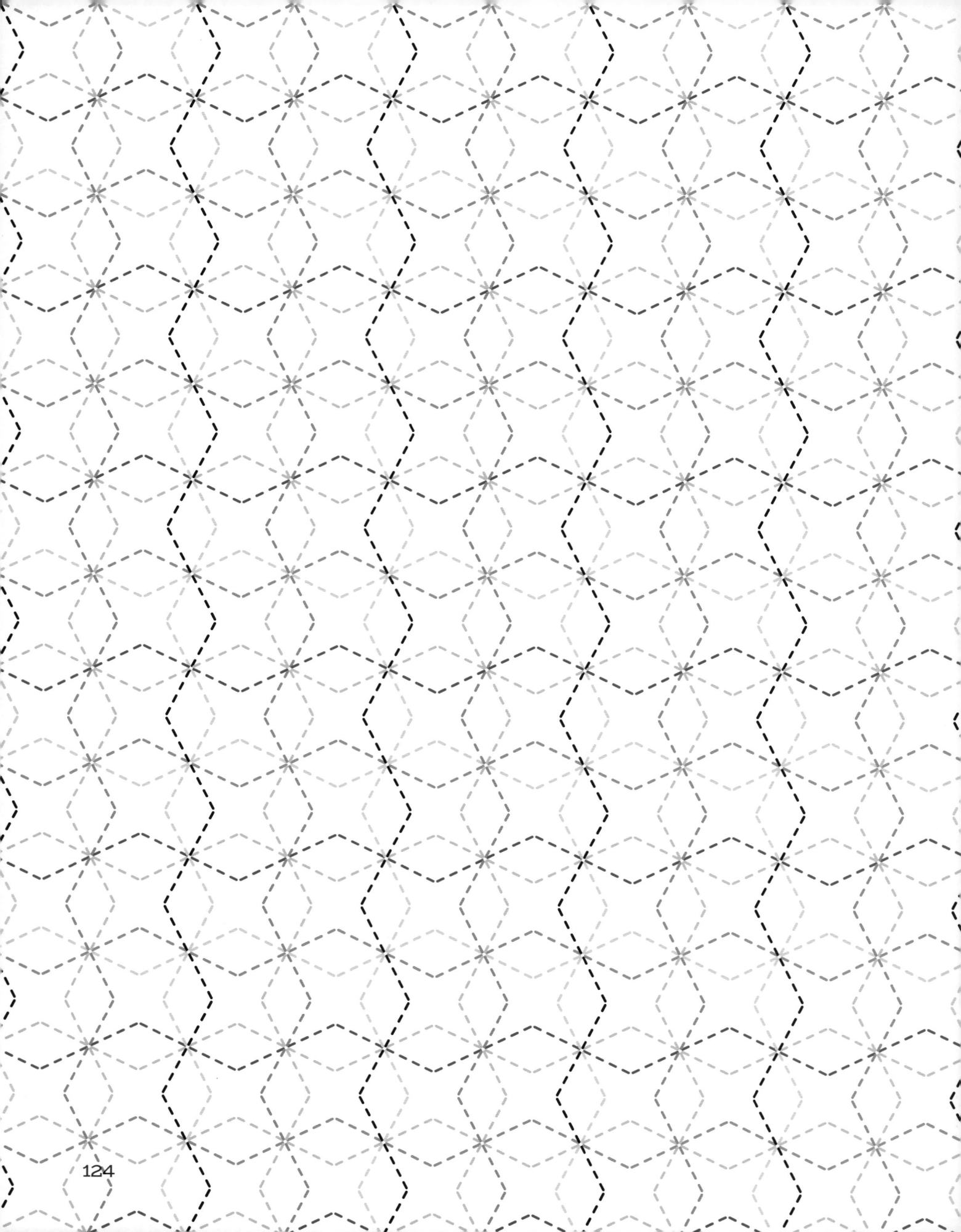

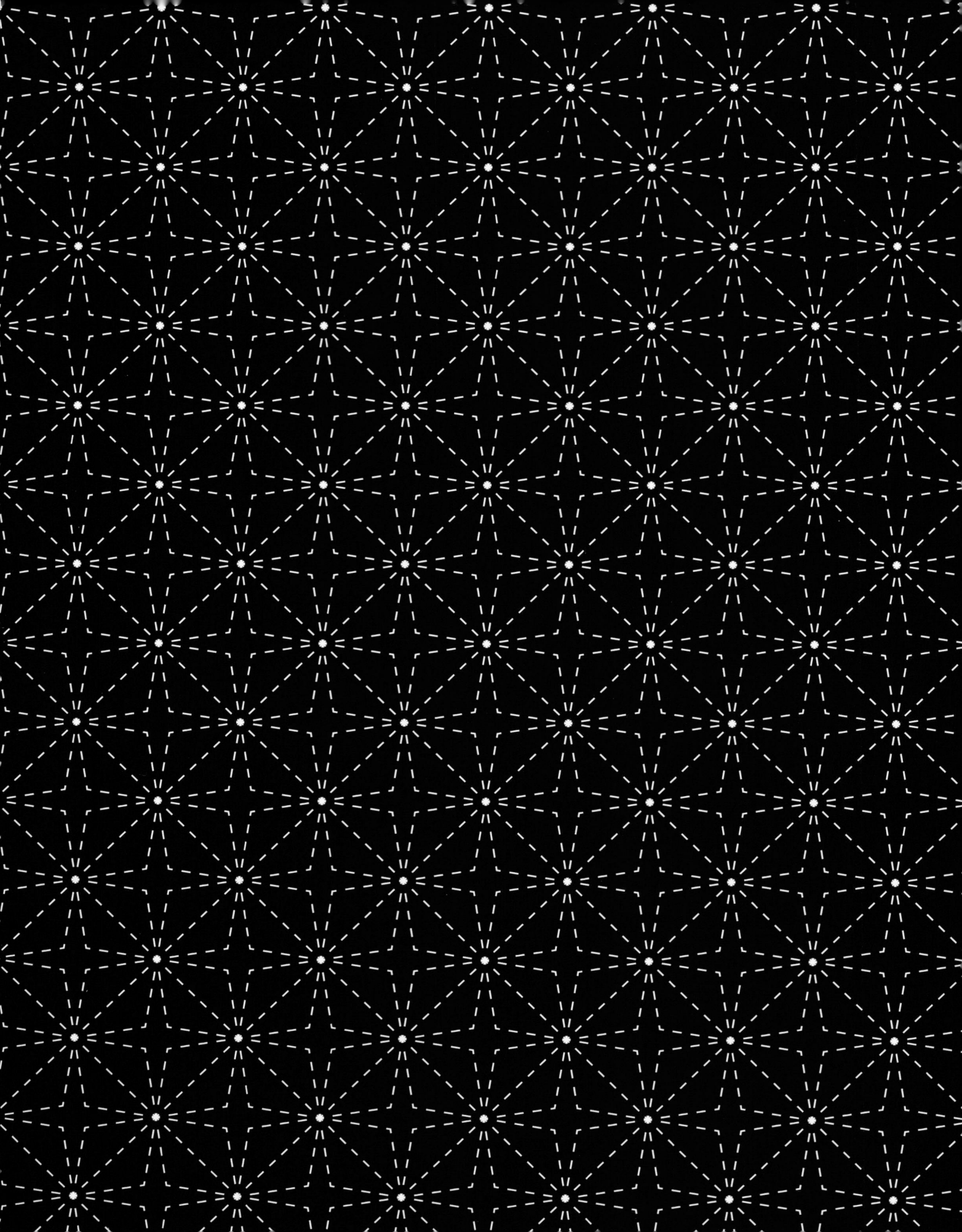

¼in (6mm) grid

⅜in (1cm) grid

1in (2.5cm) grid

Index

First published 2019 by
Guild of Master Craftsman Publications Ltd
Castle Place, 166 High Street, Lewes,
East Sussex BN7 1XU, UK

Reprinted 2019, 2020

ISBN 978 1 78494 487 2

PUBLISHER: Jonathan Bailey
PRODUCTION: Jim Bulley and Jo Pallett
SENIOR PROJECT EDITOR: Dominique Page
EDITOR: Sarah Doughty
TECHNICAL EDITOR: Vanessa Mooncie
MANAGING ART EDITOR: Gilda Pacitti
DESIGN & ART DIRECTION: Wayne Blades
PHOTOGRAPHER: Neal Grundy
TECHNIQUE ILLUSTRATIONS: Vanessa Mooncie

Colour origination by
GMC Reprographics

Printed and bound in China

To order a book,
or to request a
catalogue, contact:

GMC Publications Ltd
Castle Place,
166 High Street,
Lewes, East Sussex,
BN7 1XU
United Kingdom

Tel: +44 (0)1273 488005
www.gmcbooks.com

FSC
www.fsc.org
MIX
Paper from
responsible sources
FSC® C144853